SOCIALISM

FROM THE

CHRISTIAN STANDPOINT

THE MACMILLAN COMPANY
NEW YORK · BOSTON · CHICAGO
DALLAS · SAN FRANCISCO

MACMILLAN & CO., LIMITED
LONDON · BOMBAY · CALCUTTA
MELBOURNE

THE MACMILLAN CO. OF CANADA, LTD.
TORONTO

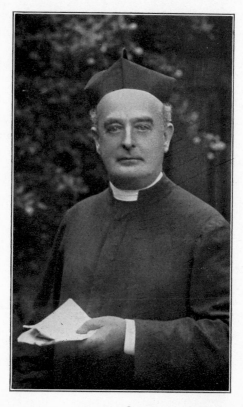

Bernard Vaughan

SOCIALISM

FROM THE

CHRISTIAN STANDPOINT

TEN CONFERENCES

BY

FATHER BERNARD VAUGHAN, S.J.

AUTHOR OF "THE SINS OF SOCIETY," "SOCIETY
AND THE SAVIOUR," "LIFE LESSONS
FROM JOAN OF ARC," ETC., ETC.

New York

THE MACMILLAN COMPANY

1912

All rights reserved

Imprimi Potest.

ANTHONY J. MAAS, S.J.,
Provincial, Maryland,
New York Province.

Nihil Obstat.

REMIGIUS LAFORT, S.T.D.,
Censor Librorum.

Imprimatur.

✠ JOHN CARDINAL FARLEY,
Archbishop of New York.

NEW YORK, November 14, 1912.

HX536
V3
C0.3

Norwood Press
J. S. Cushing Co. — Berwick & Smith Co.
Norwood, Mass., U.S.A.

DEDICATION

I dedicate this series of conferences to my many friends, in many walks of life, who, by their courtesy, kindness, and hospitality during my stay in the United States, have placed me under an indebtedness which I can never hope to repay.

The memory of my delightful visit to the States of America shall, indeed, live on in freshness, till the end of my days, while, so long as God permits me to stand at His Altar, the names of my dear friends shall rise up before Him for the fulness of His choicest blessings.

More it is not given me to do, unless it be to express the hope that, between the covers of this book they may find, not inarticulately uttered, many echoes of their own thoughts and reasonings about Socialism.

PREFACE

IT is at the earnest and repeated request of very many non-Catholics as well as Catholics who heard them, that I am venturing to publish these Conferences on Socialism from the standpoint of Christianity.

Six of the number were preached during the Lent of 1912, in Saint Patrick's Cathedral, New York. To make the set more complete, and, I hope more useful, I have added the remaining four addresses.

May I make bold to beg my readers not to forget, when perusing the pages of this book, that they are rather listening to the spoken, than reading the written, word? I do not want to "talk like a book."

These Conferences do not pretend to be exhaustive treatises on the subject with which they deal. On the contrary, they are meant to open up vistas of thought, while they themselves deal rather with the larger principles of the question than enter fully into the scholastic and economic difficulties to which they give rise.

3

To those persons who have persuaded themselves that Socialism is no menace to Creed or Country, I should like to point out that it is surely, if slowly, gaining ground, and winning clients all the world over. To-day, in Germany, Socialists command 35 per cent of the total electorate, occupy 110 seats in the Reichstag, and draw 4,252,000 votes. Besides, they hold 2000 official positions under government, and they can count on the support of all such Labour Unions as are inspired by the spirit of revolt against Capital. In the Fatherland, Socialism is a cult, a religion — a very potent factor in the life of the nation.

In France, too, Socialism is alive, active, growing, and full of enterprise. In the Chamber there are 76 Socialist Deputies, while no less than 2769 of them hold government appointments.

In England, with its 42 members of Parliament and its newly formed organization and its zealous propaganda, Socialism has already done deeds and pushed forward measures which have forced us to ask with the poet,

"Who can tell how all will end?"

Surely these facts alone may serve to remind my readers that Socialism is not "the vain thing" nor " the negligible quantity" which some writers would have us believe.

But perhaps nothing better teaches us the hold which Socialism has to-day than a study of its press.

It is the press which forms and shapes public opinion. Nobody understands this better than the Socialist. Accordingly, wherever Socialism is strong, there its press, too, is strong. In Germany, it publishes 159 papers; in Italy, 92; in France, 70; in Belgium, 56; and in England, 12. The " comrades" are thoroughly organized, they are in dead earnest, and are ready, when called upon, to make any sacrifice in the interests of their cause.

But some one will say, " Yes, on the other side of the Atlantic Socialism is, indeed, a force of growing strength, but not so here in the States. Why, it has not sent even one single ' comrade' to Congress. It has not the ear of the people." True, the Socialist Party is without a single representative in Congress, and it has failed to carry other political positions; but, for all that, we must not sit down with folded arms and flatter ourselves that Socialism has had a setback, and is becoming weak and anæmic.

Nothing in the States is more surely growing;

nothing is gathering greater strength; nothing is more violently alive to-day than Socialism.

Take what it did in New York State yesterday, election day. Socialists more than doubled their vote. In New York City they counted a gain of 12,000, in Buffalo a gain of 2400, in Rochester a gain of 200, while in all the smaller cities the vote has been twice the weight it was in 1908.

In Greater New York, Eugene V. Debs polled 33,423 votes for Presidency; an increase of 7458 on his 1908 vote.

Again, look at California. There Socialists have raised their vote from 28,659 to the astonishing figure 66,350!

To-day California leads in growth of the socialist vote, Indiana ranks second, and Wisconsin comes third. Take the country throughout, and we learn, in spite of the losses caused by the New Party, that the socialist vote has run all the way from 420,964 to 712,709.

But Socialism in the United States must not be judged only by its political vote. There is something on which it relies far more, something for which it strives far more energetically. The Socialist Party takes for its first article of faith *the printed word*. Already they are issuing 13 dailies, and are adding 4 more; they publish 350 weeklies, and are increasing that number; they own 25 monthlies and, besides, many hundred "Locals."

Socialist Propagandists are, perhaps, even more active on the "Capitalist" magazine and newspaper than upon their own. I am assured that it would be no easy matter to give a list of newspaper and magazine offices in which Socialists are not occupying responsible positions.

Certain it is that we find quite a plentiful supply of articles in our current literature written by "comrades."

Behold the platforms from which they harangue the people, and through which they enlist recruits by the thousand !

Besides relying on the written, they confide no less on the spoken word; the national headquarters maintains a staff of organized agitators under salary. Much care is also taken, and no little money is spent in training a large corps of soap-box orators, whose mission it is to orate on street corners and in the parks. In the Rand school these enthusiasts are grouped and taught their business.

The more we investigate the matter, the more thoroughly convinced we become that Socialism in the United States needs watching, lest like a sand-storm or a forest fire, a cyclone or an avalanche, it may assume proportions and gather a momentum almost impossible to deal with.

Study Socialism for yourselves as it is in your midst, and you will discover that it is "a live wire" and waiting to be switched on, "to give light," say the "comrades"; "to spread ruin!" exclaim patriots.

But even upon the supposition that Socialism was a theory in the air only, with no practical outlook at all, it would still be the duty of Catholics to point out that economically it is unsound, philosophically it is false, and ethically it is wrong. Bad in theory, it would be even worse in practice.

As Catholics, we must try and bring back to Christianity from Socialism all persons who have been smitten and captured by its plausible teachings. It is up to us "to blaze the trail," and to lead them from the desert, pathless, and barren lands of Socialism, over "the great divide," down through forests, and over foothills, into the vine slopes and the fertile valleys of the Christian Fold, to the feet of the Good Shepherd, Christ Jesus, our Lord.

In conclusion let me plead with my indulgent readers to take into consideration that these Conferences were prepared for publication between pulpit and platform engagements, and while voyaging by sea and journeying on land between the Hudson and the Yukon. Books of reference were not get-at-able *en route*. There were no libraries on the Ice-fields, none amid the Rockies. Accordingly, in some instances, I was forced to be satisfied with my notes without giving the references.

I wish to express my warm thanks to Father C. Plater, S.J., and Father Husslein, S.J., for the kind help I have received from them.

BERNARD VAUGHAN, S.J.

St. Ignatius's,
980 Park Avenue, New York,
November 7, 1912.

CONTENTS

SOCIALISM FROM THE CHRISTIAN STANDPOINT

I

SOCIALISM AND THE PAPACY

A FEW years ago, during a visit to Rome, I had the privilege of hearing from our present Pontiff, Pius X, personal, paternal advice as to what I considered my own special mission and work in life.

I was explaining to the Holy Father how my ambition was to do something for the poor workers in the slums, and at the same time help to get the truths of Christianity before those who were enjoying the better things of life. Then it was the Holy Father told me that in all I said or did I was ever to keep in mind the great principles of Catholic teaching, expounded in the Encyclicals of his predecessor, Leo XIII.

"In those Encyclicals," said His Holiness, "you will find clearly marked out the course of action that Catholics must follow in the great social movements of the day." Then Pope Pius explained how, in his own Encyclical, on Christian Democracy, published in 1903, I should find, taken from the writings of his predecessor, nineteen propositions which laid down the truths that must ever be maintained by Catholics in regard to authority and its origin, the State and its functions, the family and its duties, the rights and duties of property, capital, and labour.

So, when the privilege came to give a course of Conferences in this Cathedral, I thought I could do nothing better than follow up the thought and teaching of that great Pontiff, Leo XIII, on the various phases of the social movement, and which Pope Pius X tells us, in his letter on Christian Democracy, should be posted up in the offices of Catholic organizations, and frequently read at their meetings.

And, indeed, to whom are we to turn for light and guidance in regard to those far-reaching social questions of the time, if not to the Vicar of Him who said: "I am the Way, and the Truth, and the Life"?

I know, at once, what the enemies of the Catholic Church will say. They will say: "You are going to the wrong source for light. The sympathies of the Pope are on the side of the capitalist, and he takes little, or, at least, no deep interest in the toiling masses." This is a charge made against the Papacy; a charge repeated, insisted on, and forced upon the labouring man; it is a charge I must dispose of at the very outset of these Conferences.

What, then, let me ask you, has been the action of the Pope in regard to the bread-winners during the past nineteen hundred years, during which, as Head of Christ's Church, he has sat in the Chair of Peter? This is the question I am going to answer to-day.

Let us, for the moment, assume that the Pope, as a rule, has been on the side of those in authority. As a matter of fact, he has sometimes even lifted his hands in blessing over the autocrat. Autocrats are not much in favour nowadays. We have no use for them; and consequently some of us think that the Pope, who blessed autocrats in a day gone by, must have sided with them in their oppression of the working classes. Nothing could be further from the truth.

We must be careful not to judge of mediæval Europe as though it were a present-day civilization. There have been ages in which autocrats were not only useful, but in a measure necessary. Without them there would have been no government at all, no safety, no asylum for the weak, no protection for the oppressed. There have been times, in the dark past, when the one thing wanted was a strong hand, an effective rule to hold society from crumbling into atoms, and to defend the individual from being plundered or murdered by his neighbours. Look, for instance, at the warring Anglo-Saxons brought out of their chaos by the strong hand of the Church-supported despot of Wessex. The strong hand may have been a cruel hand, but it established order of some sort in a day when the poor man sought and craved for help of any sort.

"The feudal lord," says Lafargue, "only holds his land and possesses a claim on the labour and harvests of his tenants and vassals on condition of doing suit and service to his superiors and lending aid to his dependents. On accepting the oath of fealty and homage the lord engaged to protect his vassal against all and sundry by all the means at his command ; in return for which support the vassal was bound to render military and personal service and make certain payments to his lord. The latter in his turn, for the sake of protection, commended himself to a more puissant feudal lord, who himself stood in the relation of vassalage to a suzerain, to the king or emperor.

" All the members of the feudal hierarchy, from

the serf upwards to the king or emperor, were bound by the ties of reciprocal duties." [1] Even Hillquit, the Socialist, is compelled to acknowledge that : "Under the existing conditions of the times the class of nobility was, therefore, on the whole a socially useful class."

And so it came to pass, Popes said gracious things to various autocratic kings and domineering nobles, who some may think never deserved any encouragement at all. But does this exceptional action of the Pope mean that his sympathies were with despotism, or that he approved and encouraged the oppression of the wage-earning classes ? By no means.

The Pope has ever been the champion of the toiler, the defender of the weak, the advocate of the down-trodden, and the poor man's best friend. Cardinal Newman has well said that there is no one of those who speaks bravely against the Church to-day but owes it to the Church that he can speak at all. This is particularly true of the wage-earner. If any power can be said to have brought him into being and given him a social status, that power is none other than Christ's Vicar, the Pope of Rome.

This will appear to be an unwarranted state-

---

[1] "The Evolution of Property."

c

ment to those who are not familiar with history, or who have been brought up on history written by the avowed enemies of the Papacy. Popular literature, I grant you, is against me, Protestant fiction is against me, and non-Catholic tradition is against me, Socialists, of course, are against me, for their explanation of all changes in history is based upon economic conditions; but the writings of impartial Protestant historians are on my side.

Let me, first of all, recall a few well-supported facts, and cite a few fully recognized authorities in support of my contention. We need not go back to the beginning of the Papacy; it will be enough to start with what are called the Dark Ages — roughly, the ninth and tenth centuries of our Christian era. Alas! They may indeed be called dark, for they recall a period of destruction, of desolation, an age almost of despair. It was a time when Europe was harried from end to end by Northmen, Mohammedans, and Magyars. The very existence of Christianity, even in Europe, seemed to be threatened. The historian Gibbon, referring to it, has described a scene that actually might have been witnessed; England under a Caliph, with Mullahs lecturing in the Colleges of Oxford. Scarcely can we call the picture overdrawn. It was one that might have been enacted at that famous seat of learning.

How did Europe save herself? By the creation of a military caste. We call the rule of this caste Feudalism. Politically, it worked out as local despotism. Against it the workingman was powerless and hopeless. In those days the workingman had no organization to support him, no press to make known his wrongs, no public opinion to which to appeal. How could he, helpless, alone, on foot, with only a hoe for a weapon, hold his own against a mail-clad knight, on horseback, armed with a lance? He had to lie down and crawl under the heel of tyranny. But now all this is changed.

Consider the wage-earner of to-day as a member of a trade-union. Picture him as he stands — erect, keen-eyed and keen-witted, attending a congress as the representative of his fellows. Add up, if you will, the strong sanctions that hedge him round about; note the bulwarks that protect him. His personal liberty is secured, it is inviolate; the courts of law throw open their doors to him, the press is eager to report his words, his fellows to a man are at his back; in a word, he is welded into a strong and closely-knit organization with his brother workers. I do not, for a moment, pretend to say that his position is satisfactory, even now, but he certainly enjoys a measure of protection which not the furthest-reaching prophetic vision in the Dark Ages could have foreseen.

In the Dark Ages our brother workers were without redress when tyrannized over by the wealthy. The servant was the creature of his master, living in the hollow of his hand. It was the rule of the stronger, hard and often pitiless.

How could it be otherwise when there were no elements of cohesion among the down-trodden people, no unifying principle giving them a voice-controlling force? How was liberty, even in its most elementary form, to take root in a soil so uncompromising as this? How was Democracy to spring out of a social order in which popular initiative was an utter impossibility?

Yet, incredible as it may seem, we do find, if we turn over a few pages of later history, that the workingman is practically emancipated and is able to stand up and assert himself. He is beginning to take an active and intelligent part in the democratic government of well-nigh every country in Europe. Now, what I want to know is, how was this glorious change brought about? Whence, let me ask, came the ideas of liberty and democratic government and, more important still, whence came the motive power which gave shape and meaning to those ideas, converting them into deeds of policy and life? The answer is this: In those days, the Church had the monopoly of ideas, and whatever large and luminous ideas rose above the horizon sprang from her.

Observe, that apart from the teaching of the monks, even the mail-coated knight would have been more ignorant than the dullest of our present-day peers, while the serf could no more have launched an idea on the public than a present-day Patagonian child could write an editorial for one of our great Metropolitan papers. Any luminous ideas, which in those days flashed across men's minds and were impressed on their lives, came from the Church, and were spread abroad like sun rays from monastery and cathedral schools, which were centres of light and learning.

A religious education, incomparably superior to the mere athleticism of the noble's hall, was granted, for the mere asking, to the meanest serf. This tremendous fact alone, by proclaiming the dignity of the individual, elevated the hopes and destinies of the entire race. This humanizing machinery of schools and universities, coupled with the civilizing propaganda of missionary zeal, was the Church's work, and hers alone.

Why, her very existence amid the people was a liberal education, showing as it did that successive ages were not sporadic and accidental scenes, but continuous and coherent acts of one great and marvellous drama. "In dim but magnificent procession," as a writer reminds us, "the giant forms of empires, on their way to ruin, ceded to her their sceptres, bequeathed to her their gifts. Life became one broad, rejoicing river, whose tributaries, once severed, were now united, and whose majestic stream, without one break in its continuity, flowed on under the common sunlight, from its source beneath the throne of God."

Referring to this period a well-known Anglican historian reminds us that, "The Church was the one mighty witness for light in an age of darkness, for order in an age of lawlessness, for personal holiness in an epoch of licentious rage. Amid the despotism of kings and the turbulence of aristocracies, it was an inestimable blessing that there should be a power which, by the unarmed majesty of simple goodness, made the haughtiest and the boldest respect the interests of justice, and tremble at the thought of temperance, righteousness, and the judgment to come." (Farrar's "Hulsean Lectures for 1870," p. 115, Lect. iii, The Victories of Christianity.)

M. Guizot says: "There can be no doubt that the Church struggled resolutely against the great vices of the social state, — against slavery, for instance; . . . lastly, she strove by all sorts of means to restrain violence and continued warfare in society. Every one knows what was the Truce of God, and numerous measures of a similar kind, by which the Church struggled against the employment of force, and strove to introduce more order and gentleness into society. These facts are so well known that it is needless for me to enter into details." ("History of Civilization," Lect. vi. Cf. Balmez, "European Civilization," Eng. Trans., p. 66 *et seq.*)

But I pass on to ask whence sprang the fair flower of Catholic Democracy which put forth its leaves and flowers, and ripened into fruit in those days gone by? There was only one soil on this planet out of which so fine a thing could have sprung. That soil was the soil of the Catholic Church. Turn to the pages of history and recall who were the men who dared to stand up in Europe to rebuke the wickedness and injustice of tyrants. They were the bishops of the Catholic Church. Was it not a St. Anselm who spoke up fearlessly for the people in those days, as did Cardinal Manning, in our own time, in London?

When the great St. Thomas of Canterbury rode out of Northampton we are told that huge crowds escorted him, hung about him lamenting, weeping, for they saw in him their protector, much as in the days of our grandfathers the people of Italy flocked to greet an exiled Pope, unharnessed the horses from the shafts, and triumphantly drew his carriage, shouting themselves hoarse with their cries of welcome and love. Who, too, let me ask, was it that secured for his people on the other side of the ocean the great palladium of their liberties, the Magna Charta? It was a prelate of the Catholic Church, Stephen,— Cardinal Langton. Catholicism, I tell you, is woven into the warp and woof of all our great democratic institutions, and it is the bishops of that Church to whom Democracy stands eternally indebted.

Again, Christian teaching itself is preëminently democratic. It looks to the life to come. It points to a narrow way by which all must go, and to the narrow gate by which all alike must enter. Observe there is no "Servant's Bell" or "Tradesmen's entrance" to the Gate of Heaven. There is but one bell for all Christian pilgrims alike at the end of life's journey. If in Heaven there be any aristocracy at all, it will be the poor, the brethren of the reputed Son of the Carpenter of

Nazareth. The Church treats all her children alike; — in her ministry she recognizes no class distinctions. To say, as most socialist writers do, that the Church always sided with the ruling class is a libel on history.

In a day gone by you might have seen knight and serf bowing in the same Cathedral to receive absolution of the same priest, himself perhaps a peasant, as to-day the first of priests, the Pope, is a peasant's son. What was seen then is witnessed now, when prince and peasant unite in the same spiritual exercises.

Did time permit, it would be pleasant to recall how the sanctuary checked the hand of the smiter until the first heat of his anger and revenge had cooled down; to recall how the people gathered to see miracle plays, those moralities and mysteries which we are now trying to bring back; to recall how the foot-worn, dust-covered traveller was asked no questions as to his social position when, at nightfall, he sought the shelter of a religious house. The religious monastery or convent was, as everybody knew full well, open to all alike, to young and old, learned and unlettered, rich and poor. At Whalley Abbey, in England, standing midway between Lancaster and Manchester, and rising on the edge of Pendle forest, infested by wolves, the Cistercian monks gave free hospitality for three days to any pilgrim, whether he was prince, peer, or peasant. So freely was this service accepted that two-thirds of the monastic revenue was spent on guests. Make no mistake: altruism is no discovery of our day. It has been the sacred practice of the Catholic Church, always, all the world over. But in those days it was not called altruism, it was called Christian charity.

Speaking of the Catholic Church of those centuries, the historian Lecky says that she "laid the very foundations of modern civilization. Herself the most admirable of all organizations, there were formed beneath her influence a vast network of organizations, political, municipal, and social, which supplied a large proportion of the materials of almost every modern structure."

Let me further support my contention by citing yet another non-Catholic, Dr. Cutts, who writes: "One reason of the popularity of the mediæval Church was that it had always been the champion of the people and the friend of the poor. In politics the Church was always on the side of the liberties of the people against the tyranny of the feudal lords. In the eye of the nobles the labouring population were beings of an inferior caste, in the eye of the Law they were chattels; in the eye of the Church they were brethren in Christ, souls to be won and trained and fitted for Heaven."

I might cite a score of other authorities showing how impossible it is to read the mediæval history of Europe without being convinced that it is to the Catholic Church and to her policy and teaching, rather than to mere "economic developments," that the toiling classes owe their emancipation from slavery to serfdom, and from serfdom to liberty.

"But the Church," some one listening to me may object, "is not the Pope. What part did the Pope play in the creation of the democratic spirit?" The Church, indeed, is not the Pope, but the Church could never have defended popular liberties except in so far as she was in union with the Pope. A mere national Church can never stand up before a king on behalf of popular liberties. But in those days, called the Dark Ages, churchmen did stand up to kings and nobles precisely because their union with the Pope of Rome put into their hands a mighty power that transcended and defied all the barriers of nationality.

Had temporal lords in those days been the supreme heads of local churches, they would have retained their seats on horseback, while the serf would have remained tied to the land, without champion to plead his cause or to fight his battles. Why, the thing is going on under our very eyes to-day. What could an Erastian Church, like the Russian Church to-day, do, were it to be subjected to an attack such as that which is being levelled against the Church in France? Suppose that the President of the French Republic had been also the head of the French Church, where could the Episcopacy of France have drawn strength to oppose him and to hold their own, as they have done, to their imperishable glory? Why did the Catholic Church in my own country go under? It was because in the fifteenth century the Church in England was half Erastianized. This is why it succumbed to the tyranny of that monster of iniquity, the Eighth Henry. England was cut off from Rome. Its people could no longer appeal to a higher court. It found itself caught in a trap and severed from the champion of its liberties, the Pope.

Some of my hearers may have no sympathy with Christianity. They may be glad to see the Christian Churches Erastianized and made the tools of the secular power. I am not contesting such an opinion here. I am merely pointing out that had the mediæval Church been Erastian, popular liberties could never have been vindicated. It was the Pope that set us free.

The Rev. H. Milman, D.D. (late Dean of St. Paul's), writing of a time when anarchy threatened the whole West of Europe, and had already almost enveloped Italy in ruin and destruction, says: "Now was the crisis in which the Papacy must reawaken its obscured and suspended life. It was the only power which lay not entirely and absolutely prostrate before the disasters of the times — a power which had an inherent strength, and might resume its majesty. It was this power which was most imperatively required to preserve all which was to survive out of the crumbling wreck of Roman civilization. To Western Christianity was absolutely necessary a centre, standing alone, strong in traditionary reverence and in acknowledged claims to supremacy. Even the perfect organization of the Christian hierarchy might in all human probability have fallen to pieces in perpetual conflict; it might have degenerated into a half-secular feudal caste, with hereditary benefices, more and more entirely subservient to the civil authority, a priesthood of each nation or each tribe, gradually sinking to the intellectual or religious level of the nation or tribe.

On the rise of a power both controlling and conservative hung, humanly speaking, the life and death of Christianity — of Christianity as a permanent, aggressive, expansive, and, to a certain extent, uniform system. There must be a counterbalance to barbaric force, to the unavoidable anarchy of Teutonism, with its tribal, or at the utmost national, independence, forming a host of small conflicting, antagonistic kingdoms. . . . It is impossible to conceive what had been the confusion, the lawlessness, the chaotic state of the Middle Ages without the mediæval Papacy; and of the mediæval Papacy, the real father is Gregory the Great." (Book iii, Ch. vii, Vol. ii, pp. 100–102.)

M. Ancillon, a French Calvinist, says: "During the Middle Ages, when there was no social order, the Papacy alone, perhaps, saved Europe from utter barbarism. It created bonds of connection between the most distant nations; it was a common centre, a rallying-point for isolated states. It was a supreme tribunal established in the midst of universal anarchy; and its decrees were sometimes as respectable as they were respected; it prevented and arrested the despotism of the emperors and diminished the evils of the feudal system." ("Tableau des Révolutions du

Système Politique de l'Europe," Vol. i, Introd., pp. 133, 157.)

The German Protestant Church historian, Staudlein, says : —

"The Papacy was productive of many beneficial effects. . . . It united in one common bond the different European nations, furthered their mutual intercourse, and became a channel for the communication of the arts and sciences, and without it the fine arts, doubtless, would not have attained to so high a degree of perfection. The Papal power restrained political despotism, and from the rude multitude kept off many of the vices of barbarism." (" Universal Church History," Hanover, 1806, p. 203.)

Herder, another eminent non-Catholic writer, says : —

"It is doubtless true that the Roman hierarchy was a necessary power, without which there would have been no check upon the untutored nations of the Middle Ages. Without it, Europe would have fallen under the power of a despot, would have become a theatre of interminable conflicts, and have been converted into a Mongolian desert." (" Ideas on the History of Mankind," Part iv, p. 303. Cf. p. 194 *seq.*)

Here some one may rise up and protest : "It may

be true that the Pope was the champion of the labouring man before the Reformation, but what about the Papacy since that day?" Fearlessly Catholics may proclaim that the Popes after the Reformation, as well as before it, have been on the side of the toiling classes. Already there are large numbers of workingmen on whom the truth at last is beginning to dawn.

True, the Reformation and the Revolution swept away the old Catholic guilds and the old Catholic crafts and confraternities, but they did not sweep away the Catholic Church. She stands on the rock of ages, and not even Hell itself can prevail against her. Thanks be to God, old Catholic traditions are seen reviving to-day in the Catholic social movement in Germany, in France, in Belgium, in England, and on this vast continent of the New World. We are getting the best teaching of the Middle Ages reasserted. The social action of the Church is being renewed, and nowhere more so than on this great continent, where, under the stars and stripes, the Catholic Church is impressing upon the community the lesson that the better the Christian, the better the citizen.

The movement received new vigour when Pope Leo XIII issued his great Encyclical on Labour, which rightly may be called the workingman's charter — the Magna Charta of the working classes. That Encyclical is being preached all the world over. The American Episcopate has done much to make it known, and American citizens not of our faith are beginning to realize that the Catholic Church is the promoter of true liberty, the friend of Democracy, and the advocate of all that is uplifting to the submerged, to the oppressed, to the sweated.

Meantime, there remain many grievances to be redressed, terrible chasms to be bridged over, hideous cruelties to be stopped, and innumerable problems to be solved. I need not review the situation. It is reviewed monthly in your periodicals, weekly in your journals, daily in the press. There is no one who has summed up those evils more convincingly than Pope Leo XIII in that great Encyclical of which I have spoken.

In it he reminds the employer, in words that should never be forgotten, that in the agreements entered into by the employer and his workman "there is a dictate of nature more imperious and more ancient than any bargain between man and man, namely, that the remuneration must be sufficient to support the wage-earner in reasonable and frugal comfort." " If through necessity or fear of a worse evil," adds the Pontiff, "the workman

D

accepts harder conditions because an employer or contractor will give him no better, he is made the victim of force and injustice." What can be clearer, what fairer, what braver or nobler than a proclamation such as that !

The Supreme Pontiff, looking out from his watch-tower on the Vatican hill, sees the terribly strained state of things that has been created between Capital and Labour by the violation of this principle. Like his Divine Master, he has compassion on the multitude ; on the tens, nay, hundreds of thousands of men and women who are grinding out their lives in sweated workshops, who are huddled together in our great cities and centres of industry, who are hidden away in the cellars and attics of disease-breeding slums, and who are driven by penury and want to join the ever growing army of criminals, or at any rate of the discontented. His Pontiff's heart is moved with pity for these enslaved men and women who are our brothers and sisters in Christ, and he declares in the most solemn manner in which he can make his voice heard : "That a remedy must be found, and found quickly, for the misery and wretchedness which presses so heavily and unjustly upon such vast multitudes."

But where is that remedy to be found ? Where is

the prescription that will go to the root of the evil and cure these disorders that are threatening the very life of the social organism? I may say that I find only two physicians in the field — two, I say — who claim to have a radical cure for the disease. The Supreme Pontiff is the one, the Socialist Philosopher is the other.

The remedy pointed out by the Supreme Pontiff I will explain in a later Conference. I shall only say now that the Pope, unlike the Socialist Philosopher, has lived in close contact with humanity for nineteen hundred years, and he may be credited with knowing something about the ailment, character, and temperament of the patient. He has lived on terms of intimacy with the rich man no less than with the poor, with the children of the forest as well as with the men of great cities. No class of society is alien to him. And when class struggles have arisen and the poor have suffered, and the well-being of society has been threatened, the Sovereign Pontiff has never held back, has never forgotten his duty; he has come forward, he has diagnosed the malady, he has prescribed the remedy.

But too often has his paternal voice been unheeded. People have thought they were wiser than he. They wanted to be independent. They fancied they could find a remedy elsewhere. They said: "No, not you. We will seek our cure in Reformation and Revolution. We will seek a readier cure for our ills; we want measures more drastic than you prescribe; our sickness can yield to no treatment of yours." Thus the second condition of the patient has become worse than the first.

Now, who is the rival physician who claims that he had discovered the remedy that will go to the root of the evil? The Socialist is the man. But who is the Socialist? In what school has he been trained? What is his knowledge of human nature? How long has he been with us? What credentials does he bring? Who gave him a diploma? What has he done for humanity?

This man tells us that the cure which will right all our wrongs is to be found on the transference to the community of all the instruments of the production and distribution of wealth. We are told that this is the essence and sum total of Socialism.

If Socialism were nothing more than a mere economic proposal, independent not only of religion but also of ethics, it would never have been made the subject of a series of Conferences in this Cathedral. If Socialism were nothing more than what it is represented to be in campaign books, and on political platforms at election time, it might, indeed, be of interest to the Catholic sociologist, but it would not be deserving of the attention we are giving it in this sacred edifice. We might indeed say that it promised, without proof or guarantee, a terrestrial paradise;—that it involved a grievous injustice at the very start in the abolition of all private capital that is productive, and that, beginning with an act of injustice, it could scarcely be relied upon as the impartial dispenser of justice and right. We might say this and no more. But not so now.

Socialism is an affair of far deeper significance than a bare question of economics. It means more than the promise of a far-off fanciful Arcadia. In the words of a leading socialist writer of this country, John Spargo, it is "a philosophy of human progress, a theory of social evolution." "Our theory," wrote Engels, "is not a dogma, but the exposition of a process of evolution." "Socialism," argues Spargo, "is the product of economic conditions, not of a theory or a book." The Socialism, he tells us, that is alive in the world to-day, and upon which the great socialist parties of the world are based, is the Socialism of Marx and Engels.

The Socialism, then, that I have to deal with

is not, I say, the Socialism of the campaign book or of the political platform, but the Socialism assiduously spread among the docile working classes, the Socialism poured on anxious listeners in the Socialist Assembly Room, the Socialism scattered over the country in socialist newspapers and pamphlets, and in well-advertised editions of what are called socialist classics. I have little or no interest in Socialism as an abstract principle of economy, or as a distant Coöperative Commonwealth. My inquiry is about Socialism as a living, moving, energizing concern, with a well-organized press and a propaganda that is a marvel of enterprise, I may say, of self-sacrifice. And the question I have to ask is: Whether, everything considered, is it wiser and more ennobling for a Christian people to join in the socialist movement, or in a movement for the reëstablishment of Christian principles in the social and industrial life of a people? Shall the cry be: "On to Socialism," with all its bravery of statement and blindness to consequences, or "Back to Christianity," that has already proved itself to be the one great reforming power in the world? Of one fact we may rest assured, that there can be no permanent solution of the social and industrial problems standing out before us, till Christian principles come once more to be recognized and followed in our relations with one another. For it is nothing but the truth to say with a modern writer that "although a Christian community might abandon its faith it would still find it necessary, if it would keep clear of anarchy, to keep faithful to practical Christian principles. . . . Ultimately moral relations will have no significance, certainly no moral sanction in the minds of the people apart from the Christian principles with which they are now, or have been in the past associated." (Kelleher.) We cannot live as those who have ever "sat in darkness," and never seen "the Great Light." We can never accept the teaching enunciated by Hillquit, who, speaking for Socialists, is at pains to remind them that: "Good or bad conduct has largely come to mean conduct conducive to the welfare and success of their class in its struggles for emancipation." From all such so-called "codes of morality" let every true American shake himself free. For they strike at the root not only of Christianity, but of religion, nay, even of morality itself.

II

SOCIALISM AND THE STATE

I AM sometimes asked by letter, and sometimes by word of mouth, why instead of saying kind I say hard things of Socialism. The man in the street says to me: "If you want to champion the cause of the bread-winner, you must do something more than build clubs for him, something more than attempt to better his condition; you must even do something more than busy yourself about his little ones — you must identify yourself with his Socialism. Show the world that between Catholicism and Socialism there can and ought to be a union closer than that of wedded life itself, and then you will have accomplished something."

These questions from my wage-earning friends force me to ask: "Can the Catholic Church, the Church par excellence of the toiling classes, — have anything in common with Socialism as it is to-day; anything on which to establish kindly relations with it?" It might appear at first sight that there is much in common between them. Both protest against the evils of modern capitalism, of fierce individualism, of iniquitous competition, and of colossal wealth in the hands of the few. Read the Encyclicals of Leo XIII on the great questions of the day, and you will imagine, at times, that you are reading passages from a socialist manifesto. The working classes are described as having been "surrendered, all isolated and helpless, to the hard-heartedness of employers and the greed of unchecked competition." It is pointed out that "a small number of very rich men have been able to lay upon the teeming masses of the labouring poor a yoke little better than that of slavery itself."

Or, read again the social programmes issued by the Catholics of Germany, or of France, or of Belgium, or of England, and you will find that many of the reforms there demanded are those which figure prominently on socialist programmes.

But looking at the matter more closely, we find that a wide gulf separates the Catholic from the Socialist. Both recognize the fact, though endeavours are sometimes made to disguise it. Against Socialism, as it is, the Catholic Church has resolutely set her face. She will have none of it. Socialists, on the other hand, have declared if the ideal commonwealth is to be realized, the Catholic Church is in the way, and must go. A leading Socialist in America, once a member of Congress, has told his comrades that the last and most powerful foe they will have to meet will be the Church of Rome. I believe this to be true.

This irreconcilable antagonism between Catholic and Socialist we shall now examine. But to do so we must go outside the field of mere economics. For observe well, as I have said, Socialism, in the concrete, is not a mere economic proposal. It involves a theory of life and a view of the universe all its own, from which there is no getting away.

The first and chief difference between the Catholic and the Socialist lies precisely in this, that they hold conflicting views about the nature of civil society, and about the origin and destiny of man. This parting of the ways leads on to further problems of disagreement. The matter is so important that it demands our closest attention.

My task to-day will be to lay before you, as briefly as may be, the difference between the socialistic and the Catholic conception of the State.

Socialism is based upon the materialistic theory of evolution. This statement may be repudiated by individuals, as also by groups in the socialist body; but the history of Socialism proves my contention true. The "Christian Socialist" may protest, the pious Fabian may remonstrate, the Idealist may grow indignant; but for all that, Socialism as a living, energizing concern is not a mere economic, or politico-economic, principle; it is a growth planted deeply in philosophic and religious theories. Socialism was born and nurtured in a philosophy that denies the existence of a personal God, and that repudiates all man's duties toward his Creator. Socialism still teaches that the one true source of our social, political, ethical, and religious ideas and beliefs is to be found in the economic conditions of production and distribution of material goods. It undertakes to trace materialistic evolution from slavery to feudalism, from feudalism to capitalism, and from capitalism, through democracy, to Socialism.

Hillquit ("Socialism in Theory and Practice") tells his readers that: "The idea of social evolution is admirably expressed in the fine phrase of Leibnitz, 'The present is the child of the past, but it is the parent of the future.' The great seventeenth-century philosopher was not the first to postulate and apply to society that doctrine of flux, of continuity and unity, which we call evolution. In all ages of which record has been preserved to us, it has been sporadically, and more or less vaguely, expressed. Even savages seem to have dimly perceived it. The saying of the Bechuana chief, recorded by the missionary, Casalis, was probably, judging by its epigrammatic character, a proverb of his people. 'One event is always the son of another,' he said — a saying strikingly like that of Leibnitz." Hillquit continues : —

"Since the work of Lyell, Darwin, Wallace, Spencer, Huxley, Youmans, and their numerous followers — a brilliant school embracing the foremost historians and sociologists of Europe and America — the idea of evolution as a universal law has made rapid and certain progress. Everything changes; nothing is immutable or eternal. Whatever is, whether in geology, astronomy, biology, or sociology, is the result of numberless, inevitable, related changes. Only the law of change is changeless. The present is a phase only of a great transition process from what was, through what is, to what will be."

"The Marx-Engels theory is an exploration of the laws governing this process of evolution in the domain of human relations : an attempt to provide a key to the hitherto mysterious succession of changes in the political, juridical, and social relations and institutions of mankind." In the judgment of leading Socialists the Coöperative Commonwealth is a thing assured. You can no more hope to fight and crush it than the Indian brave could hope, with his bow and arrow, with his tomahawk and scalping knife, to fight and conquer the present-day soldier armed with the weapons of modern warfare. "The State," proclaims Professor Ward, "is a natural product, as much as an animal or plant, or as man himself."

Socialism, acting on its belief in the materialistic conception of history, expects to establish a State without reference to God. It has no special use for God. It ignores Him when it does not deny Him.

The result of this historical alliance between Socialism and atheism is that even individual Socialists, who believe in God, have assimilated certain views about the nature and functions of society which are ultimately rooted in atheism. They have broken with the Catholic tradition. They hold opinions about the rights of public authority which are, in fact, logical deductions from atheistic principles, and which cannot be held consistently by those who believe in a personal God.

I will not here deal with the blatantly anti-religious Socialist—with the whole tribe of Blatchfords and Baxes who make no secret of their disbelief in God and their desire to destroy religion. I will confine myself to the Socialists who maintain that Socialism has no religious implication whatever.

Whether they are ingenuous in so doing it is not my business to inquire. I merely wish to show that their theory of society, implicit and explicit, is directly contrary to the Christian theory of society, and that it leads to practical views as to the nature of liberty, the family, property, and so forth, which are distinctly anti-Christian.

As a sample of this fundamental error of concrete Socialism we may take Mr. Ramsay MacDonald's "Socialism and Society," a book which has gone through several editions.

We may begin by quoting the author's assurance that Socialism is not prejudicial to Christianity or family life.

"Within the scope of this communal organization of industry there will be need for smaller groups, such as trade-unions, churches, families. Indeed the larger organization will greatly depend upon the smaller groups for its vitality. As the communal organization becomes more efficient, the individual will respond with more intelligence and more character, and as the individual thus responds, these smaller groups will become more important. Trade-unionism keeping the communal organization in the closest touch with the needs of the workers; a church attending with enthusiastic care to the life, and not merely to the dogma, of Christianity; a family organization built upon a sound economic basis and serving, in as pure a form as humanity will allow, the spiritual needs of men and safeguarding at the same time the rights of the community, would be precious organs in the body communal" (pp. 212–213).

But what is this "body communal" in which the Church and the family of the future are to be snugly accommodated? The answer is unhesitating. The author sees that "a positive view of the State is essential to Socialism," and tells us that "Socialism comes with a clear and scientific idea of the aims and method of State activity, and can, therefore, discriminate between mistaken and proper methods of State action" (p. 150). In other words, as I have already pointed out, Socialism involves a certain set of principles about the nature of civil society. These principles are not Christian principles. What are they?

"The communal life is as real to him [the Socialist] as the life of an organism built up of many living cells" (p. 151).

Here we have it! Our old friend, the biological analogy, masquerading as a literal reality. Again, we read : —

"The being that lives, that persists, that develops, is Society; the life upon which the individual draws, that he himself may have life, liberty, and happiness, is the social life. The likeness between Society and an organism like the human body is complete in so far as Society is the total life from which the separate cells draw their individual life. Man is man only in Society."

"There appears to be a cell consciousness different from the consciousness of the organized body with its specialized brain and nervous system; there is a social consciousness with its sensory and motor system superimposed on the individual consciousness; both together make up the individual consciousness " (p. 18).

"In fact, disguise it from ourselves as we may, in our so-called 'practical' moments, every conception of what morality is — except neurotic and erotic whims like those of Nietzsche, or antiquated prescientific notions like those of the Charity Organization Society — assumes that the individual is embedded organically in his social medium, and that, therefore, the individual end can be gained only by promoting the social end; that the individual is primarily a cell in the organism of Society; that he is not an absolute being, but one who develops best in relation to other beings and who discovers the true meaning of his ego only when he has discovered the organic oneness of Society " (pp. 32–33).

"The chief difference between the social organism and the animal organism is, that whilst the latter, in the main, is subject to the slowly acting forces expressed in the laws of natural evolution, the former is much more largely — though not nearly so largely as some people imagine, and in a less and less degree as it becomes matured (another organic characteristic) — under the sway of the comparatively rapidly moving and acting human will. This gives the former an elasticity for change which the other does not possess. But the type of its organization, the relations between its various organs and the mode of their functioning — and it is with these alone that I have to deal in this book — are biological " (p. 37).

Here we see one of the root fallacies of Socialism. It is held consistently by those Socialists who are materialistic evolutionists; and it is held more or less unconsciously by those Socialists who undertake to find room for "the Churches" in the socialist régime. The fallacy consists in mistaking a very useful analogy for an identity; in resolving a moral life into a physical or physiological process.

E

Hillquit, to quote an American Socialist, assures us that : —

" The historical and uniform course of the evolution of the State and its overwhelming importance as a factor in human civilization have led the school of thinkers, of which Auguste Comte, Saint-Simon, and Hegel are the typical representatives, to the opposite extreme — the conception of the State as an organism. The 'historical' or 'organic' school sees in the abstract phenomenon of the State a concrete and independent being with a life, interests, and natural history of its own. To these thinkers human society is a social organism very much like the biological organism. The social institutions are so many of its organs performing certain vital functions required for the life and well-being of the organism itself, while the individual members of society are but its cells. Mr. M. J. Novicov, probably the most ingenious exponent of the 'organic' school of sociology, carries the parallelism between the social organism and the biological organism to the point of practical identity, and Mr. Benjamin Kidd, criticising the utilitarian motto, 'The greatest happiness of the greatest number,' says: 'The greatest good which the evolutionary forces operating in society are working out is the good of the social organism as a whole. The greatest number in this sense is comprised of the members of generations yet unborn or unthought of, to whose interests the existing individuals are absolutely indifferent. And, in the process of social evolution which the race is undergoing, it is these latter interests which are always in the ascendant.'"

"In short," Hillquit concludes, "the State is the end, the citizen is only the means."

The biological concept of society by no means originated with Socialists. It is found in St. Paul; it has been used by Aristotle, by St. Augustine, and by St. Thomas. We come upon it even in the Encyclical on Labour. But observe a Catholic when using the idea always remembers that he is dealing, not with a literal fact, but with a useful analogy. To accept the idea as more is to rob human life of its value, to destroy liberty, and to put an end, not merely to revelation, but to human personality itself. At best man becomes a mere function of the social organism, a muscle or nerve centre in the body politic — with no free or independent soul of his own.

The Catholic, I repeat, in using the comparison has always realized that he was dealing with an analogy, and not with a literal fact. To accept this biological idea as an analogy is to get a truer insight into the nature of society; to accept it as a literal fact (as does Mr. Ramsay MacDonald) is sheer nonsense.

Society is a moral organism. What do I mean by that? I mean that it resembles a physical organism in some important points, and differs from it in other points no less important. Hence, what is true of a physical organism cannot be straightway applied to the organism of society.

A physical organism seems to be dowered with autonomous parts with specific activities, united by a superior directing principle. But this is not really so, since the vital principle is the only source of life. The members exist entirely for the body; their activity is ordained *directly* for the common good. In a moral organism there is also autonomy of parts and unity. But the autonomy of the parts is *real* and not apparent. The individual in society has his own individual end, directly given him by God. He is answerable to God alone, not to society except in so far as society is delegated with God's authority. The individual will be judged not merely as a member of society. He is not wholly immersed in society. Society exists as we shall show in order to protect him and to help him to do certain things which he cannot do for himself.

To say, then, that we are all members, or limbs, or cells of one organism is to use an analogy supplied by St. Paul, and is helpful so long as we remember we are using an analogy. If we go on to argue that we are as wholly dependent on society for our life and destiny as the cell is dependent on the organism, then we are talking nonsense.

Catholics, in their union with the Church as well as with the State, realize that they are members of living organisms. As a Catholic, I recognize myself to be a member, a cell if you will, of that mystical Body of which Christ is the mystical Head. As a citizen, no less I realize that I am also a member of another organized society called the State. But not for a moment could I even imagine that in consequence of my relationship to State and Church I had lost my personal identity, my personal liberty, and, consequently, my personal responsibility. Neither by the Church nor by the State have I been swallowed up and assimilated. Were I to shake myself free altogether of the State, or of the Church, or of both, I should not thereby cease to be. My own individual life might still pursue an aimless career ; indeed I should be answerable to God for having cut myself off, by a misuse of liberty lent me, from two institutions, one of which is necessary for the development of social life, while without the other, what could be man's life spiritual?

By all means let us talk of ourselves as cells of a living organism called the State, but let us know what we are talking about, and let us keep clearly before our minds the not unimportant fact that we are using the term in a sense not identical with, but only analogous to, that in which it is used of a human body or of an animal. Man does not exist merely as a cell in State organism. He is not merely what the eye, the hand, or the foot is to a human body. He is complete in himself, and were he to find himself alone on a desert island, he would still be, in a very literal sense, a self-determining being, responsible after life to God for the things done in the body.

Now, this fundamental misconception of the nature of the State as a real, live organism, in which man is but a cell, is, as I have said, widely diffused among Socialists. It colours their practical proposals, and it shapes their views of the individual, of the family, of liberty, and of property. This glorification, this apotheosis of the State, is not without its entertaining, its humorous side, if it were only profitable to dwell on this aspect of the case. To judge from socialist writings one would be almost led to think that the new State was to be some god in disguise, or at least the ideal superman; whereas, as a matter of fact, when cleansed of its war-paint and stripped of its stage clothes, it might be found to be only a large coöperative body of political office-holders, whose symbols of office might be an axe to grind, a purse to fill, and whose motto might be: "We are the State."

The State, even as we know it, is muddlesome and meddlesome enough. Under Socialism, into what kind of Oriental Despotism would it be perverted? In a House of Bondage, such as it might be, man would have about as much opportunity of realizing himself as a slave in the open market. He would be, as we have shown, but a cell, a nerve centre, a muscle in the all-absorbing State organism. He would be free neither to choose his occupation nor to determine where to exercise it, nor to employ labour on it. Would his house in any true sense be his home? Would his children belong to him or to the State? Would he be free to provide for them, or to exercise parental rights over them? Would he be a self-determining citizen, or, on the contrary, a State-crushed creature only, bound up in red tape, labelled with a "food ticket," and with a State-appointed occupation and a State-given destiny?

Again, what under Socialism would happen to the man who was wronged by the State and sought redress? I do not know that he could appeal to law, because all the lawyers would be State officials; I am not sure that he could write to the press, because all newspapers would be owned by the State. The only thing left him might be anonymous letters, the resort of the knave, coward, and fool.

I can picture nothing more deadly dull than life as it might be under a socialist State. You cannot think of it without there rising up before you the vision of some reformatory, with inmates garbed in a drab uniform, and moving to and fro in dull monotony.

In spite of what many Socialists tell us, it is very difficult to conceive of the socialist State except in terms bureaucratic.

Perhaps Ansley's picture of it may, after all, be quite as true as Spargo's.

Certainly Herbert Spencer, whose philosophy so many Socialists adopt, has drawn for us from socialist teaching the "Coming Slavery," which cannot be made to fit in with descriptions of the Coöperative Commonwealth described by writers of the Hillquit school — Bellamy, Morris, Gronlund. "The Socialist State," writes Hillquit

("Socialism in Theory and Practice"), "is not the slave-holding state, nor the feudal state, nor the state of the bourgeoisie — it is a Socialist State."

That is about all that can legitimately be said about it, for as yet the working plans of this Elysian State have not been submitted by Socialists for our inspection. Before attempting to do so let them determine whether State and municipal ownership, on a large scale, has succeeded both politically and economically; whether the State-owned railways of Europe are superior in every respect to the private-owned railways of America.

As to land, we are assured that no socialist commonwealth would oppose its occupation and possession by persons "using it in a useful and *bona fide* manner without exploitation."

The small farmer would not find his acres confiscated nor his occupation gone under a socialist government. Perhaps not, but conditions might be laid down, the fulfilment of which would mean that all interests in his occupation would be gone. What farmer is going to live on his land and cultivate his farm, unless he can employ labour, realize his stock, and put by a bit of money for his old age, and for those to come after him? Alas! Socialism betrays, at every step, a plentiful lack of knowledge of human nature.

Let Socialists follow the farmers, with their thousands of dollars, going forth yearly to take up land in the States and in Canada. Let them ask these enterprising folk what is their aim and object in so doing.

They will soon discover that the farmer is not to be satisfied with tilling, ploughing, sowing, and reaping to secure a mere livelihood. He means to put money by, to enjoy the fruits of his labour, and to have a bank account with which to set up his sons and daughters in positions of respectability, comfort, and ease. He wants none of your Socialism. We must not forget that in treating of the socialist State we are dealing with a condition of things which, according to the Marx-Engels teaching, is, as Kautsky observes, "not the product of an arbitrary figment of the brain, but a necessary product of economic development." The Coöperative Commonwealth will evolve after the socialization of all the means of production and distribution, when all men will be fellow-workers, when all men will be contented with their lot, when all men will cease to be jealous or ambitious, when exploiting will have forever ceased, when the gewgaws, baubles, and toys of this world will no more enchant and ravish the soul with happiness. In a word this Elysian, this Utopian Industrial State will be realized when man shall have ceased to be man with a mission in this world and with a destiny in the next.

"It has not yet come," exclaim the sanguine followers of Marx and Engels, "but come it will, and then the happiness of all will be as the happiness of each, — supreme, complete, and lifelong."

Having briefly sketched an outline of the socialist State, which we are assured is on its way to bring men contentment and peace, let me now put before you the Catholic view of the State. What is the nature and character of the State? What are its distinctive functions, its rights, and its duties?

The word "State" has various meanings, two of which are to our purpose here. In the wider sense of the term a State is simply a community of men organized for all purposes of civilized social life. Minor organizations are set up for subordinate or local interests only. Not so the State. A State sums up all the relations of the various groups of which it is composed which have to do with temporal well-being. I say with temporal well-being, for the State has no direct concern with man's eternal interests and destiny. In this wider sense, then, the word "State" simply means not a society, but society itself.

But the word "State" is also used in a narrower sense, signifying civil authority, as when we speak of State interference, State monopoly, obeying the State, and so forth. I shall employ the word "State" in the restricted sense, with occasional excursions only into the wider meaning of the word. Let me, first, set forth the Catholic view of the State, and then we shall be in a position to consider in what points the socialist idea is in conflict with it. The Catholic view of the State, I need scarcely remind you, is based on belief in the existence of God. God the Infinite, Eternal, Almighty, All-wise, and All-loving Spirit has created man, has dowered him with intelligence and free-will, and set him on this earth to work out an eternal destiny. Man not only belongs to God inalienably, but depends on God utterly for all that he is and has. Nothing belongs so utterly to man as man does to God. Man has been sent here for a purpose, and that purpose is to carry out God's will. This world is his temporal place of probation. It is man's drill-ground rather than his playroom, his school rather than his home. This life is not an end in itself, but a means to something better. It is not the play, but the rehearsal; not the terminus, but the journey; not the landing stage, but the outward voyage. In this life man has to fit himself, with God's help, for his eternal destiny. He must reach the goal by the exercise of his faculties, but more especially by the exercise of his self-determining will. He must work out his own salvation. No one else can do it for him. He can appoint no deputy. To God, and to no one else, man must give an account of his stewardship, and at any moment his Master may ring him up.

To pass on. Man, the individual, no matter whatever may be said of his supernatural life, is not self-sufficient as regards his temporal welfare. He must associate himself with others for mutual help and support. Man is a social animal, and only in society can he live a full and healthy human life. Cut off from society, he is stunted and warped. His faculties have no opportunity of free play, his being cannot expand nor his talents unfold. This fact is so generally admitted that I need not press the point. Civil society, then, has been established by God to supplement individual activity, effort, and enterprise.

"No main tendency," it has been once said, "of human nature can have its fulfilment except under some social organization. If learning is to flourish among men, there must be learned societies; if religion, religious societies." Hence, too, civil society, or the State, is needed for the protection and promotion of the temporal interests of its compound integral parts.

If you ask me what sort of civil authority does God, the Founder of society, demand, I reply that God leaves men to determine that for themselves, in accordance with their special needs and circumstances. There is no distinctive blessing on Monarchy any more than there is on Republicanism. All that God commands and nature enjoins is government; that is, effective government, suited to the needs of the particular people in question. Observe, there is no divine right of kings, but there is a divine right of a government. This or that form of civil authority is the work of man. Civil Authority itself is the command of God. It is required by nature. It is in every legitimate sense of the word natural.

Here let me call your attention to what constitutes the range or field of State action. I want to make it clear to you what is its "natural" sphere of operation, but before answering this question, I want to remind you for what purpose the State exists, what is its final cause, why precisely it has been called into existence. Time does not permit me to pause and review the ideas of the old-fashioned liberal political economists who, influenced by Kant, held that the State had merely an external and negative purpose, that it existed simply in order to protect men's liberties. "Leave men alone," it said, "keep other men from interfering with them, let each man be free to pursue his private interest, and the result will be a grand social and economic harmony." This view of the State, propounded by Liberalism, is the very antithesis of that promulgated by Socialism. The one unduly restricts the action of the State, the other unduly exaggerates it. With neither can the Church come to terms. Against both she utters her protest. Both she emphatically condemns.

Catholic economists remind us that the State exists for the purpose of securing the public well-being; that is to say, the State is summoned into being and is set up to secure that complexus of conditions which is required in order that all the organic members of society may, as far as possible, attain to that temporal happiness which conduces to their ultimate destiny.

Briefly, then, the State has two purposes to accomplish. It has to protect man's rights; and it has to assist him to do what he cannot do for himself, but what, at the same time, he requires to do if he is to lead a normal, happy life here on earth, preparing him for a happier one still in Heaven. The old-fashioned Liberal says that the State has nothing more to do than to protect man's legitimate rights. The Socialist says there is no limit to what it can and may do; while the Catholic says that the twofold function of the State is to protect man, and to assist him to do what he ought to do, and yet what without State help he cannot do. As St. Thomas, following Aristotle, well says, "Men form societies not only to live, but to live well."

The State, then, has for its mission to assist its members to realize themselves as civilized members of society. The State exists not for the sake of particular individuals, not even for particular classes, but for the general good of all. The State supplements the efforts of the individual; it caters for the general good.

But here it may be objected that the State does sometimes make special provisions for particular classes or groups of individuals. It builds and maintains hospitals, wherein the sick have their individual wants attended to, and from which the healthy are excluded. It boasts of its "garden cities," and its city homes where the people and the poor find shelter. It supports lunatic asylums for which the sane have no use. In a word, the

State, as a matter of fact, does a number of things for the benefit of particular classes. All this is true, and if we keep carefully in our minds the distinction to be made between absolute public goods and relative public goods, we shall discover that the State is fulfilling the function for which it was called into being. We must bear in mind that the State acts in order to secure public welfare, either absolutely or relatively. It has no direct mission to make each individual or any particular family rich, happy, and prosperous; but it helps where a man cannot help himself, provided that by so helping the individual it at the same time furthers the common interest and temporal prosperity of the whole community.

The State protects. About this all are agreed, with the exception of anarchists. Observe how transcendental this function of the State is. The State may rightly do things which no individual can rightly do. It may say of parents who are grossly neglecting their children: "I will take these children away from these particular parents, for if I do not, the rights of children to life, liberty, and a decent livelihood will be altogether violated." Similarly, the State may interfere in private workshops, where the toilers' lives are in danger by insanitary conditions; where they are crippled by

F

iniquitous hours, or stunted by a sweated wage. Again, the State is obviously called upon to settle disputes, to repress vice, to take measures to prevent the commission of crimes, and to protect the rights of its citizens.

But what about the duty of the State to assist its citizens? As I have already pointed out, the State must help them to do what they ought to do, but what unaided they cannot do. To borrow the language of M. Baudrillart, its business is not *"faire* nor *laissez faire,"* but *"aider à faire."*

The State exists in order to secure both "negatively" (by protecting liberties) and "positively" (that is, by giving assistance) the general temporal well-being, and this both absolutely and relatively.

With regard to economic matters the civil authority must facilitate the production of wealth, and avoid obstacles to such production, for example, excessive taxation. It must stimulate production. It must encourage domestic sanitation, hygienic training, technical education, and so forth. It is not the function of the State to distribute wealth itself, for such wealth it has not directly produced. But it may by wise legislation see that the distribution of wealth is conducted according to the laws of equity and justice. Negatively it is called upon to repress crime against religion and morality and to punish public scandals, while positively it must support and protect what tends to establish, develop, and fortify morals and the public exercise of religion.

Observe, however, that the State is not concerned directly with the morals and religion of individuals. The State is not a religious teacher, or a guide in theology, or a direct means to supernatural well-being. That belongs to the province of the Church. Our law courts are set up, not to try sins, but crimes.

Some one may ask me, What are the absolute limits to State authority? To this I answer, the State has no right to interfere directly, save when its action is necessary to the general welfare. It may not touch private rights. It may not interfere with private activities, save when the public well-being requires it. In other words, it can only touch men in so far as they are citizens or members of the State. And let us never forget that besides being a member of the State, man is also a moral being, with inalienable personal rights and an eternal destiny. It falls within the province of the State to stop the individual from selling, say, improper pictures or scrofulous literature. It may punish him for purveying fraudulent food-stuffs. A thousand other things demanded by the public well-being falls within the province of the State. The State is set up by man, not man by the State.

It were needless for me to remind you that there are some things the State may never presume to do. It must not enact laws contrary to the laws of our Creator. It may not interfere with religious freedom, or with parental rights, unless it be to protect, as I have already pointed out, the essential rights of children. I might continue, but I have said enough to make it clear, that there is no taint of Socialism about the principles which I have laid down. According to the Catholic view, the intervention of the State in the play of social activities is never justified by mere utility, but by moral necessity only. The State, for instance, has no right to say, "I will assume the direct control of all mines, for then the miners will be better off;" but it has a distinct right to say, "I will assume the control of industries which are sweated, for in no other way can I secure the rights of the sweated worker;" in other words, State interference is justified only when private initiative becomes insufficient. The State must look to the well-being of the whole social organism.

Again, let me insist that if we keep in mind the

fact that the State exists chiefly to supplement private initiative, then the scope of State interference, instead of widening and deepening, should on the contrary automatically diminish in proportion to individual and class initiative and enterprise. Why this? Because, thanks to the wise supplementing of initiative by the State, individuals will become more and more capable of looking after themselves and their own interests. According to the Catholic view, the State is like the parent who teaches her growing child to walk, while on the contrary, according to the socialist view, the State is like the foolish mother who keeps her growing child in a baby carriage, giving it a bottle to keep it quiet.

Such, in brief, is the State as viewed from a Catholic standpoint. There are two extremes to be avoided — a foolish distrust of State authority, calculated to prejudice the common welfare, and an exaggerated confidence in State action, which would stunt private initiative, check enterprise, undermine liberty, and suppress character.

In conclusion let me ask you never to forget that the State, as we understand it, is not the "output of mere economic conditions," it is not "the dynamic expression of material evolution," but on the contrary it is a God-given Institution resting on private property for its material foundation, resting on the family for its natural foundation, and resting on religion for its spiritual foundation.

Let no man, let no body of men, dare to attempt to undermine these sacred foundations without which no State could long endure the ravages of time, the passions of men, the shocks of war. Remember ever that the State's first and most important duty is that of not meddling, not obstructing, not taking over to itself "all income-producing property," not hampering the rights, activities, labour, and genius of its citizens." It should remember that it is set up for no other purpose but to protect and to promote the well-being of the whole community; to supply its deficiencies, and to assist its many weaknesses. The State exists for man, and not man for the State. It is the man and not the State that matters; it is the man and not the State that is endowed with a human soul; it is the man and not the State that is called to an eternal destiny. The State must never forget that prior to it, both in nature and in time, is man and the family too, to safeguard whose interests and to promote whose welfare it has been called into existence. That is its destiny. It will take the State all its time to discharge its own mission, to fulfil its own functions, to do its own work, keeping ever steadily before it this never-to-be-forgotten truth, that the individual does not exist for the State, but the State for the individual. These are principles brought out most forcibly and developed most beautifully in the great Encyclicals of Leo XIII, to which I have so often referred.

There are two volumes which I should like to see in the hands of every Catholic American citizen — in one hand those Great Encyclicals, in the other the Great Constitutions of his country. With these two works to guide, uplift, and inspire him he would become a power in this New World for the propagation of those principles of truth and liberty, before which Socialism, with its all-absorbing State, would vanish as Darkness before Light.

III

SOCIALISM AND THE INDIVIDUAL

ALL noble and lofty human action presupposes the influence of some high ideal, for no healthy human life can long endure unless sustained by some such uplifting force. Hence it comes that men who have fulfilled great missions in this world have done so under the guidance and stimulus of an ideal. Take Washington, or Napoleon, or Gordon, or Cecil Rhodes; they were men of action, inspired and actuated each by his own overmastering ideal. People who begin by losing their ideal end by losing their work. That man cannot live by bread alone is true now as always, and hence it is truly said that "the policy that has no ideal will never vitalize a people."

Your reading of history will bear out what I have said, and you will indorse the words of a modern writer who reminds us that: "The only test of progress which is to be anything more than a mere animal rejoicing over mere animal pleasure is the development and spread of some spiritual ideal, which will raise into an atmos-

72

phere of effort and distinction the life of ordinary man." ("The Heart of the Empire," C. F. G. Masterman, p. 30.)

Even a man of light and leading among Socialists, Keir Hardie, is forced to confess that: "A labour party without an ideal cannot last. There must be a Holy Grail," he says, "which they are ever in search of, which they are making sacrifice to reach, and which will inspire and enable men and women to do mighty deeds for the advancement of their cause." (Speech at Belfast, *vide* Hunter, *l.c.*, p. 127.)

Mr. Keir Hardie, of course, looks to Socialism to supply such an ideal. Of its powerlessness to do so I shall have something to say presently. What I wish to note here is that he too admits the need of a high ideal, and as so often happens, even with anti-Christians, he borrows his metaphor from mediæval Christianity. It is, indeed, a storehouse rich in ideals.

"The imperious need of to-day," says a writer in *The Times*, "is ideals. At no time has there been a greater need for ethical and spiritual ideals than now, when on all sides the material things of life are apt to assume undue prominence."

All then agree that man must have an ideal. The purpose of this Conference is to show that

Christianity does, as a matter of fact, offer the one satisfactory ideal, by the acceptance of which alone modern Democracy can hope to develop along sound and healthy lines. Socialism — despite its Utopias, its rhetoric, and its appeal to the imagination — does not supply such an ideal. In Christianity lies the hope of Democracy. In Socialism lies its peril, its ruin.

For Democracy has now to make its choice. Will it have living Christianity, or will it have living Socialism? It cannot have both: the two ideas are mutually exclusive. And one or other it must take, if it is to have any kind of a complete ideal, any theory of life. Of course it may have partial and departmental ideals of various kinds, such as the ideal of Imperialism, or the ideal of Municipal Efficiency, or Physical Culture, or Popular Art. But these things do not fill the whole canvas of life, or group together all man's aspirations into a single dominating aim. They cannot enter into every department of man's life, or illuminate every phase of human activity, or inspire the whole man with enthusiasm. We are driven by an instinct of our nature to seek for an all-embracing formula, and this, so it would seem at the present day, must be either Socialism or Christianity. There is no third competitor that

I can point to at present in the field. We cannot fall back on pure individualism. Man is a social being and cannot find his happiness in isolation, in a cold-air compartment, apart from the happiness of others. He must have an inspiring object of devotion. He must contribute to the happiness of others. The old individualistic philosophy is gone, gone forever as a discredited system. So far as Socialism has recognized this reassuring truth, Socialism deserves our warmest approbation and thanks. "In so far as Socialism is a protest against extreme individualism," writes Father Cathrein, S.J., "Socialism is perfectly right." ("Socialism," p. 305.)

But Socialism, like the lady in "Hamlet," "protests too much," or rather its protests have led it to an exaggeration which is almost as harmful as the exaggerated individualism which it attacked and defeated so thoroughly. For its tendency is now to lose sight of the claims of the individual altogether, to subordinate the individual to a Leviathan State, to change him into a bolt, or cog, or crank in its machinery. And not only does it overlook the individual, but it overlooks the present. This is a matter of great importance, and later I must be allowed to consider it at some length. Socialism in its reaction against a false individualism has rejected that true individualism which is the necessary basis of a sound Democracy.

Something has been said already about the socialistic idea of the State. We have seen that to the Socialist the State (or, if you prefer it, the Community) is everything, while the individual is very little indeed. The Socialist tells me that I am a mere cell in an organism, and that my individuality is valuable only in so far as it contributes to the welfare of the social organism. I have already pointed out that this view, based as it is upon a misunderstood analogy, robs human life of its value, and deprives man both of his sense of personal dignity, of his independence of character, and of all incentive to self-improvement and self-development.

We are living in a day when we must be on our guard against forgetting or ignoring the claims of the individual, or to put it in the language of Christianity, against forgetting man's immortal soul. There is a natural tendency to submerge the individual in the social organism, and to lose sight of his paramount rights, because of the seemingly larger claims of the community. Cardinal Newman, in a sermon on the Individuality of the Soul, has a passage which it will not be out of place to quote here. It luminously brings out what I want so much to insist on, that the individual must, in the present scheme of things, be given his right place — man is a distinct and separate existence, not a screw only in complex State machinery.

"Nothing is more difficult," writes Newman, " than to realize that every man has a distinct soul, that every one of all the millions who live or have lived is as whole and independent a being in himself as if there were no one else in the whole world but he. To explain what I mean : Do you think that a commander of an army realizes it, when he sends a body of men on some dangerous service ? I am not speaking as if he was wrong in so sending them ; I only ask in matter of fact, Does he, think you, commonly understand that each of those poor men has a soul, a soul as dear to himself, as precious in its value as his own ? or, Does he not rather look on the body of men collectively, as one mass, as parts of a whole, as but the wheels or springs of some great machine, to which he assigns the individuality, not to each soul that goes to make it up ? "

"This instance," continues the writer, "will show what I mean, and how open we all lie to the remark, that we do not understand the doctrine of the distinct individuality of the human soul. We class men in masses, as we might connect the stones of a building. Consider our common way of regarding history, politics, commerce, and the like, and you will own that I speak truly. We generalize, and lay down laws, and then contemplate these creations of our own minds, and act upon and towards them as if they were the real things, dropping what are more truly such. Take another instance : when we talk of national greatness, what does it mean ? Why, it really means that a certain distinct, definite number of immortal, individual beings happen for a few years to be in circumstances to act together, and one upon another, in such a way as to be able to act upon the world at large; as to gain an ascendency over the world, to gain power and wealth, and to look like one; as to be talked of and to be looked up to as one. They seem for a short time to be some one thing; and we, from our habit of living by sight, regard them as one, and drop the notion of their being anything else. And when this one dies and that one dies, we forget that it is the passage of separate immortal beings into an unseen state, that the whole which appears is but appearance, and that the component parts are the realities. No, we think nothing of this: but though fresh and fresh men die, and fresh and fresh men are born, so that the whole is ever shifting, yet we forget all that drop away, and are insensible to all that are added; and we still think that this whole, which we call the nation, is one and the same, and that the individuals who come and go exist only in it and for it, and are but as the grains of a heap or the leaves of a tree."

If we are to avoid the Scylla and Charybdis of extreme Individualism on the one hand and of extreme Collectivism on the other, it is imperative for us not to forget the personal equation, the individuality, the personality of a human soul. Its distinctness, apartness, wholeness in itself — Man is man because of his soul, not of his citizenship.

But my complaint is not merely that Socialism would subordinate man to the State, but that it would subordinate him to some future State with a very problematical existence, of a very doubtful character, and which might prove to be the most cruel tyrant that ever ground an individual into the dust. Clearly it might be so. Socialism seems to lose sight of the fact that true individualism is a necessary basis of sound Democracy. It proposes to subject man to a State, the product of socialist fancy, forgetting to recognize man's own individuality, personality, and worth.

"Why care about your own career?" it says

to the individual. "Your career is to provide a career for those yet to come. Your reward must be to labour for generations not yet born." "No one," says Bebel, "has a right to consider whether he himself, after all his trouble and labour, will live to see a fairer epoch of Socialism. Still less has he a right to let such a consideration deter him from the course on which he has entered." ("Woman," Eng. Trans., p. 264.)

All such idealism as this implies a pitiful disregard for the constituent elements of human nature, and goes to show that Socialists, who make a problematical future State man's ideal in life, have either smuggled religious sanctions into their programmes, or else are insulting the intelligence of their audience.

For a moment note the inconsistency of the socialist position. He rails at Christianity for "dealing in futures," and deluding the people with a "draft on Eternity," yet he himself speculates in futures of a far less assured character than the heaven which even a shoeless child, selling the evening paper in a slum, knows to be the term of his earthly pilgrimage.

Socialism insists that the ideal which it lifts up to its followers is both scientific and valuable. I maintain that it is neither the one nor the other.

I have already pointed out how unreasonable and misleading is the Socialists' application of biological analogies to human society. Such analogies have their uses, but when unduly pressed, they turn to absurdities. They rob man of his identity, of his personal equation, of his rightful status among his fellows, converting him into a chattel, a wheel, nay, into a mere cog in State machinery. Nor is the ideal which it advocates valuable. We must never forget that man is an end in himself, that he must not be made a mere means to the welfare of others. It cannot but be pernicious to lift up before him false and debasing ideals.

No human ideal can be valuable, can stimulate to action, can call forth a man's best energies, which denies or ignores the worth of the individual man. Democracy, after many years of struggle and protest, has banished that pagan principle summed up in the words of the poet Lucan, *Humanum paucis vivit genus*, — the human race exists but for the few. Christianity has taught Democracy the wickedness of such a maxim, and has helped them to toss it aside. "No," says the Church, "each individual here and now as well as hereafter has his value and must be considered. He has his personal work and must have his per-

G

sonal reward for its accomplishment. He is an end in himself and must never be made a mere means to the welfare of others."

Socialism takes Lucan's maxim and repeats it in a no less objectionable form. "*Humanum futuris vivit genus*," — the human race lives for a problematical future. This is a denial of the worth of the individual here and now, which is even more sweeping than were the principles of the Roman slaveowner. He at least held that there were some men on earth, however few, who were to be regarded as ends in themselves. Somebody, at all events, he thought, was getting the advantage of human society. If the many were having a bad time, the few, at any rate, were enjoying themselves; if some were being crushed beneath the chariot wheels of tyranny and pleasure, others were being borne forward to goals of highest human ambition. But present-day Socialists, on the contrary, must be content with the "wait and see" policy of which we have lately heard so much.

The ideal offered us by Socialism is the Commonwealth State with the voice of its comrades for the law of its life. The ideal offered us by Christianity is a life penetrated and permeated with the spirit and the principles of Christ.

And I say that my first quarrel with Socialism

is that it makes too little of the individual and too much of the State. It is a sort of deification of the State. For the Socialist the State is practically everything, while the individual is practically nothing at all. I notice that Socialists are told by one of their foremost representatives that the State is as essential to the individual life as the atmosphere, without which man cannot live.

"The being," they are told, "that lives, that persists, that develops, is society. The life upon which the individual draws that he himself may have life, liberty, and happiness is the Social State."

What we are to think of this analogy so elaborately drawn out, I have already said in my last Conference. We have to put it down, taken literally, as sentimental nonsense. It is sheer nonsense to speak of the State as if dowered by a vital principle such as exists in a human body. The State has been called into being and set up, not to appropriate but to protect, not to absorb but to assist the rights of man. The State is not a person, in the strict sense of the word, it is a thing only, an institution, with its limitations.

But what, let me ask you, must be the upshot of putting before Democracy an ideal which offers no immediate satisfaction to man's needs, but only the hope of a vague, problematical future? The upshot is bound to be this — a policy of grab. Human nature has no patience to wait for joys to be realized in some future State about which there is no certainty. It demands a present instalment of justice; it will have it at any price, even at the price of bloodshed and a Reign of Terror. If our people are taught that it is right to deprive private owners of their capital, they will press for immediate confiscation. They will themselves take the short cut to justice; it is even now becoming hard to hold some of them back. As a matter of fact, can we blame them? If their hope lies in a socialistic kingdom, if their paradise is to be found somewhere here on earth, the sooner that kingdom is realized, the better for them, and the sooner they pass into it, the sooner will they attain the real human happiness which is their end of life.

In Alaska, where Socialism seems to thrive among the miners, very recently I met a miner returning home from his shift. He had been known to me in the north of England, and at that time he was a practical and devout Catholic. Meanwhile he had been got at and had enlisted under the red flag. In course of our conversation this comrade told me he had no further use for religion of any kind; that Socialism was his cult. He had made the discovery that until all the instruments of production and distribution were socialized there could be no hope of heaven, but hell only. He assured me that most of his mates were of his mind, and were determined to convert the hell made by capitalists into a socialist heaven. There was none other. In it no class distinction would be found, and there would be one sin only, rebellion against the sovereign will of the people. He was fed up on the grossest of materialism. His hope was the socialist State. — It was his ideal, his worship, his religion.

Now for a moment let me point out to you how very different from the socialist ideal is the ideal of Catholicity. She offers to the individual, no matter what his stand on the social ladder, something more tangible, more definite, more immediate, more worth having than anything dangled before the eyes of the comrade Socialist. Taking the individual by the hand, the Catholic Church says: "I value you. I esteem your own personal worth, and I watch with untiring delight your success, which is certain if you care to make it so. You have a personal equation, a personal life, a personal mission. You are dowered with an immortal soul, and your destiny is as glorious as it is enduring. To attain your end you must, in a word, realize yourself; you must fulfil your divine mission. That is what I care about. To attain your destiny you must love your fellow-men and work for their spiritual and temporal advantage. Listen to me, and I will show you how to make the world a better and a happier place for your having been in it. I will teach you your duties to your neighbour. You will take your place in the great battle between light and darkness. Your love of Christ will lead you to combat injustice, to promote charity, to uplift the downtrodden, to stamp out sweating, to make life possible, and to make penury and misery impossible. And your reward will be, not merely the thought that future generations will be happy, though it will, indeed, include the thought that you have helped to bring true happiness within reach of the many. Your reward will be that you have done that which you were sent to do, and that you have secured your right place in the Kingdom where personal merit meets with a reward too which shall be personal, though at the same time social. You will not have flung yourself away for others. No, you will have saved your own soul and made the best of even your own self, — for yourself and for others. God's grace will be your comfort and your strength in this life. His presence and His glory will fill you in the world to come. Because you will have done His work and fulfilled His designs in you, His word to you will be: 'I am thy reward exceeding great.'"

This is a message that a Christian people can understand. This message, and this alone, will teach them restraint, will bear them up and on, and give them courage. Nay, this message alone will make them truly unselfish. And it will be a source of real comfort to them when they need it most.

Socialism may be stimulating enough to the active young man who finds a positive physical exhilaration in making perfervid speeches to appreciative audiences. It may attract the men whose experience of the world's heartlessness and cruelty has made them bitter and discontented. It may appeal to University undergraduates who seek for what is new, and for what smacks of generosity, and creates notoriety; to bored people who are looking for a fresh sensation with which to whet their jaded appetites. But what can it do for broken men and women who are preparing to face eternity? What can it do for the strong man smitten down by a hopeless and lingering disease? What can it do for the woman who is faced with the prospect of carrying a poignant sorrow to her grave? What can it do for the thousands of our fellows who are without hope in this world? Small comfort to them to dream of a time when others may fare better. They want to feel sure of the strong arms of the Everlasting God about them, and to know that they, too, are to share with Him His triumph over sin and death. They want to feel assured that their pains bravely borne, their duty manfully done, their failures patiently accepted, are not to be the mere condition of some one else's temporal happiness (on the Socialist's own showing they are often not even as much as this), but on the contrary that they are to be the recognized accomplishment of the work which they were sent to do, and for which an everlasting personal reward awaits them. In a word the people, the man in the street, and the purveyor of goods, all of us want an ideal. He may know it not, but in reality man's need is Jesus Christ.

The true Christian is one who follows Christ and the teaching of Christ with a measure of enthusiasm. There is no philosophy of the Academy, or of the Porch, or of the Garden which can pretend to compete with Christ's method of making the most of a disciple — of making the bad man good, and the good man better. If you want to cultivate not natural virtue merely, but charity and chivalry also, you must leave Plato and Socrates, Kant and Spencer, and enlist in the service of Christ. Philosophy may indeed act as a finger-post on the roadway of life, it may indicate to you the way to a naturally good, that is, to an unself-ish, state of life, but it can do no more. It is without equipment to lay hold of your mind and heart; it has no personality by which to capture and captivate you, no living, inspiring example with which to vitalize and actuate you spiritually.

What poor humanity stands most in need of, I say, is an ideal that will uplift, sustain, and vitalize all its senses of body and powers of soul. In other words it needs the leadership and the ex-ample of one who is more than a chieftain to his clan, more than a captain to his troop, more than a king to his court, more than a lover to his bride. There is one such ideal and one such only, and His name is Jesus, the Saviour.

"It was reserved for Christianity," writes the rationalist historian Lecky, "to present to the world life's highest ideal — Jesus Christ, who is not only the highest pattern of virtue, but the strongest incentive to its practice." Humanity to-day wants the mind, the heart, and the will of the Master, Jesus Christ. It needs His patience with a Nicodemus, His delicacy with the Samaritan, His sympathy with a Magdalen, His tolerance with the harlot, His forgiveness of a Peter, His mercy to a thief; it needs His methods of going about doing good; having compassion on the multitude; with a mind open to see, with a heart open to feel, with a hand open to give. Christ, with His principles of justice and charity, is the Social Reformer of whom the world stands in need to-day. Behold here, then, your ideal, your pattern of virtue, and your incentive to practise it.

The immediate end set before you is a life permeated through and through with the spirit of Christ, the remote end, union with Him in paradise.

I shall be told by not a few ardent Socialists that the teaching of the Christian Church about other-worldliness makes men indifferent about securing decent conditions of life for others in this present world. The Christian Church, they contend, encourages squalor and stagnation, and is an obstacle to national prosperity and progress. It cares for the self-regarding virtues only, neglecting all altruistic tendencies.

Such charges as these would not deserve our attention were it not for the wide extent to which they prevail in the popular press. The author of that admirable book called "The Key to the World's Progress" has, I think, made it clear that the Church has been, at least indirectly, a most powerful promoter of material civilization, and this in three ways. First of all, she has put before men ideals which are the condemnation of the seven deadly sins, in which are included covetousness, sloth, and idleness; secondly, she has taught men the dignity and duty of labor, reminding them that "in the dim morning of society Labour was up and stirring before Capital was awake," placing before them the picture of Christ in the workshop at Nazareth; and thirdly, she has been the unfailing upholder of family life upon which material civilization and true progress depend.

What more glorious chapter is there in the history of the last two thousand years than the record of Christian charity? Turn back to the earliest ages of the Church and you will find her bishops and priests and laymen erecting institutions for widows and orphans, captives and debtors, slaves and poor. You will find the Church struggling to abolish slavery, giving dignity to labour, improving the condition of the workers, protecting the weak and feeble, taking the lead in religious and secular education and in all social reform.

And her spirit is still active. To take but one page of this glorious story, let me point to my fellow-Catholics in England to-day. We are a small minority of the nation,—perhaps one in seventeen. We have (through no carelessness of our own) far more than our proportion of poor. We are strangled by the expense, unjustly imposed upon us, of paying immense sums for the education of our children. In two dioceses alone we have spent upwards of a million pounds of our own money in building schools, and many thousands on their upkeep. Yet in spite of all this we have made inconceivable sacrifices, both in money and in personal service, on behalf of the poor, the suffering, and the afflicted. I would ask my readers to turn to that last edition of the "Handbook of Catholic Charitable and Social Works" (Catholic Truth Society, 69 Southwark Bridge Road), where they will find a perfectly amazing record of the work that has been done in England alone (at the cost of God knows how much self-sacrifice) by our priests and nuns, our religious orders, our devoted laymen and women. They will read of a score of homes for the aged poor, of fifty homes for boys and girls, nearly as many orphanages, fourteen homes for penitents, hospitals for consumptives and for the dying, reformatory schools, refuges and rescue societies, shelters and soup-kitchens, — but the list is interminable. This work is done by men and women who shun publicity and who labour in the face of overwhelming difficulties. It is done in many cases by men who have given up brilliant careers in the world for the sake of doing work like this: by delicately nurtured ladies who have put on the rough robe and adopted the severe rule of the Sisters of Charity or the Nazareth House Nuns in order to follow Christ more closely by rendering loving service to His poor. I have spoken of the good works done by the Catholic Church in England only. I might multiply these a hundred fold by citing similar works of mercy done in other lands, notably in the United States of America.

I am not now arguing with those who maintain that all these duties should be undertaken by the State. I am arguing with those who say that the Christian ideal makes men selfish and indifferent to the wants of their suffering brothers. And I say that their contention is a falsehood which is abundantly disproved by the facts which I have quoted, by others which I might quote.

And I say, moreover, that Socialism has no such record to show us. Where can it point to a similar unselfish solicitude for human sufferings? It has spread much bitterness abroad ; it has fostered discontent. But what has it done to heal the wounds of humanity? What has it done to wipe away its tears, to mitigate its pains, to console its death-bed?

"By their works you shall know them." True there is need for justice as well as charity. But the promoting of social justice is enjoined upon us by our Christianity no less than charity; and the socialist protest against charity shows quite an extraordinary ignorance of the deepest needs of human nature. Charity, in the Christian sense of the term (and not in the cold, humanitarian sense which the word has come to bear in these days), will always have its necessary place in the world. The world without it, no matter to what perfection of material civilization we might attain, would be a sorry place to live in, a desert without an oasis, a land without sunshine. Democracy knows this well enough in its hours of sober reflection; and those who endeavour to fill its ears with cheap and cowardly gibes against those who have given their lives in the service of Christian Charity are doing the world but a poor service, while they are giving their own cause away.

But let me turn to another point of contrast between the socialistic and the Catholic ideal. The Socialist urges that Christianity paralyzes enterprise. On the contrary I answer that it is Socialism that paralyzes enterprise and Christianity that fosters it.

Why are men enterprising? It is because they feel that they are taking part in a struggle, with the hope of ultimate victory, in a cause which is worth fighting for. If any of these conditions be absent, men's enterprise will fail them and their efforts relax. Before you can get men to work for a cause you must convince them that the cause is in some sense a "good" one, that their efforts will promote it, and that they will have a share in its ultimate triumph.

Now it does not require a very extensive acquaintance with history to convince us that, in modern Europe at any rate, the only source of unflagging enterprise among the people is the Christian religion.

Of unflagging enterprise, observe: and among the people. There may indeed be found apart from Christianity a feverish and short-lived enterprise among the people, just as, apart from Christianity, there may be found unflagging enterprise among the few who have the advantages of wealth and leisure, of intellectual interests, of a promising career in some field of human endeavour. But you will not get unflagging enterprise among the people unless they are moulded by the spirit of Christianity.

Why is this? The reason is very simple. A wave of prosperity, the opening up of new fields of industry, imperialist sentiment, — these may for a time occupy the popular imagination and stimulate to action. But we all know how, with the supplying of man's material desires, comes the growth of fresh desires, of insatiable desires. There can be no limit, no ultimate satisfaction in this direction. Progress in material improvement, unbalanced by a corresponding growth of character, means an ever growing discontent.

Material improvements will not of themselves improve character. They are rather a test of character, a snare to character. The mere possession of good things does not teach us how to use them. It merely multiplies our temptations to abuse them. To teach us to be honest, just, restrained, unselfish, we must be inspired by motives strongly set in religion. For these we must turn to Christianity. Socialism does not even pretend to supply them. Like the wisest human philosophy it finds such a task entirely beyond its reach. So it falls back on the comfortable assumption (which is dead in the teeth of history and common sense) that when people are all made comfortable, they will be freed from their passions, they will become upright, noble, good.

This reassuring doctrine does not find much support in fact. Experience does not go to show that people become better in the measure in which they become richer. As a matter of fact they do not even become kindlier, gentler, or more sympathetic with those they have left behind. Where wealth accumulates, says the poet, men decay. If you want to come across refinement, content, and buoyant hope, you must leave the palaces of pleasure and the mansions wherein is found "idleness and fulness of bread," and pass out into the homestead of the Breton, or the châlet of the Tyrolese, or into a cabin in Connemara; there if your eyes are open, they will fill with tears to see the spiritual wealth and rare beauty of those children of God who have none of the prizes of this life, none of its luxuries, and not much of its necessaries. One day as I stood talking to my friend Bridget Joyce in the far West of Catholic Ireland, a smart motor whistled past and was soon lost in a cloud of dust.

"Well, Bridget," said I, "and what do you think of that? Do you feel envious of that gallivanting lady?"

Turning to me she replied: "Maybe, Father,

H

that when I reach heaven I will give her a start and pass her myself, never mind the noise and the dust.''

I might multiply incidents so typical of Catholic peasantry to whom heaven and the things beyond are a much more intense reality than any gewgaws so highly prized in this life.   Let me give another little story proving my point that it is not material well-being that is the first necessity for contentment in those who recognize that they are the creatures of God.   Not long ago I called to see a bed-ridden mill-hand friend of mine who was being cared for by a sister, the wife of a worker in a spinning district in the north of England.   To my surprise I saw for the first time a seventh child, a crippled boy about seven years of age, among her brood in the kitchen.   Incidentally I discovered that besides the bed-ridden sister this crippled urchin had been given a home in this workingman's four and sixpenny per week cottage.   When I expressed my enthusiastic appreciation of this surpassing kindness and goodness, the woman, who was scrubbing her floor, looked up and said: ''It's nought much to be proud of, Father; yon cripple was spoiling to death where he was, so I thought I'd care for him myself, knowing as if God could provide for six, He wouldn't let us go short with a seventh." But what need is there of adding to this list which might be drawn out to any length, to prove that it is not what you have but what you are that really matters !

The comfortable doctrine that passions fall away in proportion as comforts arise is an assumption which reminds me of the proclamation of the so-called Knowledge School, — that man, by becoming scientifically wiser, becomes morally better. Truth to tell, between the scientific triumphs over nature and spiritual victories over self there is no necessary relation at all.   In the laboratory there is to be found nothing to neutralize the poison of human passion ; in the observatory nothing to correct the aberrations of the soul's light ; in the surgery nothing to heal the wounds, or to mitigate the pains of a broken or aching heart.   Scientific culture, like material prosperity, has no moral sense. It is not from the microscope nor from the magnet, nor from the scalpel, nor from the telescope, nor from any other scientific instrument that man learns the secret of changing his heart and of stimulating the pulses of his spiritual life.   There is one, and one instrument only, that can enlighten the mind, subdue the will, and tame the heart, bringing to the eyes compunction for the past, and to the whole being resolution for the future, and that instrument is the Cross of Christ: "*Ave, Crux, spes unica.*" The weapons of knowledge may indeed serve to make the material world better, but if we want to improve the moral world, we must draw its amendment from the Crucifix. If the Figure on the Cross will not appeal and move a would-be-Christian people, then nothing will.

To aim, then, at the improvement of material conditions without taking thought for the improvement of character is, in the long run, to defeat one's object. For a time things may go well enough; the new interests may keep men occupied and absorb their energies. But by degrees their enterprise will become feverish; they will deteriorate in spirit and temper. Social life will become an impossibility, for men will come to regard material resources as the one aim of life. Society will turn into a great game of grab, terminating in results of which some of us already see the tokens. Self-indulgence, not self-forgetfulness, will then become the order of the day.

"But," objects the Socialist, "you are inconsistent. You have just been objecting to Socialism on the score that it tells men to be unselfish and to work for the coming generation. Now you object to it on the ground that it leads to self-indulgence."

I answer that the two charges are perfectly consistent. Socialistic principles overlook the individual here and now, and endeavour to base themselves on an unreasonable altruism. Socialistic practice, on the other hand, does foster just that glorification of material success which, as I have said, must end by defeating its own object and paralyzing enterprise.

The rank and file of the men who belong to socialist bodies do, as a matter of fact, care little about generations to come. They will have the good things of life now. They want here and now to pass into their Commonwealth, their earthly paradise. "Every man standing in practical life," said August Bebel at Erfurt in 1891, "knows that it is not by our ultimate goal that we have attracted these thousands. Of our ultimate goal they are only too ready to say, 'What is the good of our working for a goal that we shall perhaps never live to see?'"

This is a somewhat startling admission from the recognized leader of Socialism in view of his declaration, already quoted, that such seeking for immediate results is deserving of all censure. But this admission can be matched by the statements of many other socialist writers who have in similar fashion given their case away. Listen, for instance, to Horace Gronland: —

"It is to the discontented wage workers that the Socialist can appeal with the greatest chance of success. . . . The masses of men are never moved except by passions, feelings, interests." ("The Co-operative Commonwealth," p. 184.)

So the upshot of all these boasted altruistic socialist principles is to be an unrestrained rush for "the Promised Land." What effort is being made to train the people, to give them a sense of responsibility, to teach them restraint? The socialist leader, having enunciated his theory as to the pure disinterestedness which all men should practise, gives them not the slightest reason for practising it, but holds up to them, as the supreme ideal, a picture of mere material well-being. He then leaves "the discontented wage-earner" to secure the carrying out of the plans. To get his self-denying ordinance put into execution he appeals to "passions, feelings, interests."

It is not difficult to foresee what must be the result. The carrying on of the socialist State would demand a very large measure of altruism. This quality, so far from being increased by practical socialist propaganda of the more thoroughgoing type, is being rapidly diminished. Hence Socialism is fostering a selfishness which would make it impossible to carry out their scheme of things for a single day. You cannot grow figs of thistles.

Were Socialism really producing in men the unselfishness and nobility of character without which the socialist State could not be got to work, it would demand our utmost respect. But, then, it might become obvious even to Socialists themselves that the socialist State would not be needed. Were we good enough for the socialist State, we should be good enough to do without it! But the fact is that Socialism is not making men any better. It cannot do so as long as it limits its horizon to the improvement of material conditions, sets up its heaven on earth, and recognizes no morality but self-interest and class-hatred.

Very different are the principles and practice of Christ's Church. She begins with no disparaging remarks about the valuelessness of the individual. She tells every man that he is an end in himself, that he is of unspeakable worth, that he has an immortal soul. No matter what his fortune or his position, by doing his duty he can make his life a triumphant success. Yes, he has duties to his neighbour, — to his neighbour's soul first, and then to his neighbour's body. He must labour as a good soldier of Christ, and as a good citizen, to remove injustice from the world. He must take his share by legislation, by personal service, by enterprise of every kind, in order to improve those conditions of life which reduce his fellow-men to abject poverty, disheartening and crushing them and making them incapable, morally speaking, of living a Christian life. The Christian whose religion is a living actuality to him has a perpetual stimulus to beneficent activity, a constant spur to unselfish enterprise, a lasting motive to works of chivalry and charity. Because he believes in a life to come, he will help to make this world a better place; because he loves Christ and sees Him in all his fellow-men he will serve all men. He will value influence and power because they give him increased opportunities of doing God's work. He will value knowledge and science, literature and art, health and culture, both in himself and others, because all these things are the reflections of God's wisdom and bounty, goodness and beauty.

He is heir to all the ages and the brother of all mankind. His interests extend to all human action, for God's interests are everywhere involved. Above all he has a permanent motive for enterprise, — and his enterprise will be marked by a restraint, a balance, a sureness of direction which will make it of inestimable value to the world.

His enterprise will be unflagging because he is

not fighting a losing battle. Socialism has not begun to score yet; the Socialist, who is consistent to his principles, has to admit that for all men now living life is a ghastly failure. Not so the Catholic Church. She is winning her victories and gathering in her harvest every day and all day long. Every day many hundreds of her children meet death under every imaginable circumstance, — in youth, in old age; in poverty, in prosperity. But the Church does not pause to question what has been their material success in the past. The great question for her is not how much they had a year, but how much they are going to have for ever. Have their lives been a victory for Christ? Have they done their work in the world? Have they fulfilled their mission in life? They may have contributed some little to the cause of social reform; poor things, they had enough to do, it may be, to find a bare living for themselves and their little ones. They may have been pariahs of society, — "problems" in their own persons, inmates of workhouses, or dwellers in the slums, or invalids in garrets. But their lives were precious in the sight of the Eternal Wisdom, and they will reap their reward and wear their crowns, — else, indeed, their lives were a failure. Cardinal Newman has described their supreme hope with a master hand. It is a poor dying factory girl who speaks : —

"I think if this should be the end of all, and if all I have been born for is just to work my heart and life away, and to sicken in this dree place, with those mill-stones always in my ears, until I could scream out for them to stop, and let me have a little piece of quiet, and with the fluff filling my lungs, until I thirst for one long deep breath of the clear air, and my mother gone, and I never able to tell her again how I loved her, and of all my troubles, I think, if this life is the end, and that there is no God to wipe away all tears from all eyes, I could go mad."

I know I shall be told by the followers of modern ethics that we ought to do right for right's sake, and that to introduce any system of reward or payment is stimulating action to a low moral plane. These preachers of high spirituality do not seem to me to know much about the humanity with which I come in contact. Right for right's sake is what I call fair-weather ethics. Tell the man driven mad by passion, or tell the woman carried away by emotional feeling, to remember right for right's sake, and they will not so much as pause to listen to you. They will give you the slip with a smile of contempt for you and your silken-thread maxims. Truth to tell, under the burning pressure of passion man, and woman no less, needs the strong sanction of strong morality. Your undogmatic lay morality is but a theory; it cannot cope with difficulties, it imparts no loftiness or strength of mind. It is at once shattered in the stern conflict of good and evil.

For a moment pause and consider how the hope of reward is the great stimulus to human action. Among other characteristics which mark off man from the lower creatures there is this: that whereas they work without any object or end in view, man as man always acts for an object, or, as our Lord puts it, for a reward.

The beasts that perish eat, or walk, or toil, or sport without any sort of accompanying reflection. They live in the moment, and for the moment, neither looking before nor after. Theirs is a mechanical action, to which they are moved by instinct, impulse, or necessity, as the case may be.

Man, on the contrary, no matter whence his origin, no matter whether he be native of a civilized land or barbarous, no matter whether lettered or ignorant, religious or profane, Christian or heathen, always proposes some object to be obtained, or some danger to be avoided by his action. So true is this, that those actions alone are termed *actus humani*, human acts, which are inspired by some reward or good to be attained, whereas those actions which proceed from impulse or necessity are merely *actus hominis*, the actions done by a man, but not manly or human actions properly so called.

Man's reason imposes on him this necessity in all he thinks, says, or does — some object to be secured. The action itself may be bad, may be immoral, may be fraudulent, still he proposes some imagined reward to be obtained by it. Men do not sin for sin's sake alone. Or the action may be in itself indifferent, as walking or riding, or painting or drawing, but there is still some object; or it may be trivial, a mere exercise of muscle, such as rowing or leaping, but yet even then there is still an object in view. Or again, it may be good in itself, as almsgiving, or praying, feeding or nursing the poor, instructing the ignorant. No matter what the action is which happens to be engaging a man's time or attention, if he is a reasonable being, he will be moved to do it by the hope of some reward unless it be a pure love-act.

This reward may be near or remote, it may be attainable or unattainable, it may be good or bad, earthly, temporal, sordid; or heavenly, eternal, and divine; whichever it is, it never ceases to inspire and actuate the work done.

Now let us consider for a moment what it is that determines in any particular case the reward a man proposes as his object.

It is nothing without, outside of man, for nothing can touch and force a man's will. You may physically force a man's limbs. The martyrs were often, by brute force, compelled to offer fire and water to the false gods of the heathen; their bodies were thrown to wild beasts; but their wills could not be forced. Not even God Almighty forces a reluctant will. For He has imposed a law on Himself, He has given to every man a free will, a will unfettered, and in the hands of man are life and death. In his own choice is the object for which he will contrive and labour in the sweat of his brow. If he toils for a reward from God, he shall receive one "exceeding great"; if he labours for a reward from men, he will secure one scarcely worth having.

Once more I ask: Does experience go to show that the higher a man mounts the social ladder, the stronger becomes his attachment to his fellows left below? The prosperous man in the city, even more than his poor brother in a slum, needs the uplifting force of a great ideal to save him from becoming self-centred.

Behold, then, the two rival ideals presented to

you by Socialism and Christianity. The former regards this life as an end in itself; the latter recognizes it as a preparation for a life to come. Both may agree, to a large extent, in their actual programmes of social reforms; both may help, if they will, to make life less bitter to our hewers of wood and drawers of water. Both may unite to wipe out the slumdoms of our cities, helping to make life more human by setting up a better material environment.

We must not forget that the State is a natural institution with well-defined rights and duties, limited by the prior rights and duties of the family and of the individual. Socialism, on the contrary, is an economy set up to run counter to the purposes for which the State, under the providence of God, was instituted. Under Socialism State action, instead of being supplementary to individual action, would become a substitute for it. The individual would be swallowed up by the State; he would be no more than a cell in its great organism.

This I declare to be an inversion of the natural order. Socialism is non-natural if not unnatural.

For a moment let me develop this contention. Socialism would thwart and cripple many of those natural desires and aspirations in man which should be by all means fostered and developed. Socialism would paralyze his freedom.

The Socialist will resent this and say that man is not free at present, that he is broken on the wheels of a cruel industrial system, and that he never will be set free till Socialism is triumphant.

For all this I repeat that under a socialist régime man would be a slave, not a free man. Even though he had plenty to eat and drink, and wherewith to be clothed and wherein to find shelter, he would in no true sense be free. Free he could not be because he would not be master of his own life and destiny. Under Socialism no man would have the ordering of his own life. He would be but a cog in the State machinery, and as much under State control as an electric switch in the hands of its owner. Man would be a slave. I admit that, owing to abuses that have crept into the present-day sytem, man is limited in his choice of vocation in life. Under Socialism he would have little or no choice at all. His own life would not be his own. The liberty-loving citizen would not be free. He would be crushed out of existence. Under Socialism there would be no use for anybody who was not bound to the State as his supreme Lord and Lawgiver.

Man would be policed by one supreme public authority. His life, his talents, his activities, his aims, wishes, and aspirations would all be laid on the altar of sacrifice, consecrated to State service. How would this suit the American citizen, who if there is one thing he almost worships it is his freedom and independence? Why, thousands upon thousands in this great Republic have come over here from the other side in order to escape what Socialism wants to increase and multiply — the network of red tape, the snares and naggings of officials who, at home, robbed life of its atmosphere of freedom. But not only would man, under a socialist State, have no opportunity of ordering his own life and exercising his own personal freedom, but under Socialism he would find no scope for the expression of that desire of owning productive property which is natural to man, all the world over. This most legitimate desire, inherent in our race, is a natural instinct which would be strangled to death in the hands of a socialist Commonwealth.

Like the Socialist the Christian recognizes the modern evils of capitalism, but he would abolish these evils not by making control public, but by making use common. "Whosoever has received from the divine bounty," says Leo XIII, "a large share of temporal blessings, whether they be external or corporal, or gifts of the mind, has received them . . . that he may employ them as the steward of God's Providence for the benefit of others."

According to Catholic teaching the State has no direct and immediate power over private property, but it may, when public well-being requires it, step in and reconcile its mode of acquisition and its use with the common good. The right of the State is a power of jurisdiction falling directly on the individual, indirectly only on property. If the old Catholic laws about property and the obligations attaching to it were once more brought into general practice, we should find ourselves many milestones nearer to a solution of our present-day social problems.

Alas, both in principle and in spirit Socialism and Christianity differ widely, and are, in fact, altogether beyond hope of embracing common lines and motives of action.

Again, I must insist that I am speaking of Socialism as a living movement, "as a philosophy of human progress and as a theory of social evolution," and not as an economic proposition only. There is nothing anti-Christian in the idea that all capital may be owned by the community, if it can be lawfully acquired from the individuals

I

and managed for the common good. If Socialists could show that all private productive property could be made the property of the State without the violation of any individual right, and managed without danger to man's spiritual or temporal welfare, there are many earnest Catholics who might join hands with them on the question of common ownership. But this is not the question I am discussing. It is Socialism as a going concern, as a practical movement, as an energetic propaganda, as an actual energizing enterprise, as a new ethical view of life and morality that I am considering.

And I say that historically its cause is inextricably bound up with anti-Christian postulates; its ideal is the State, and it worships the State as its maker, as its god.

Which of the two ideals, let me ask you, will satisfy the deepest needs of Democracy? Which of the two ideals I have presented to you, Christ or the State, will help to make men less discontented, and more humane; which will teach men to become pure, and brave, and true, loyal in life and death, just and merciful, generous and chivalrous; in a word, which will inspire them to be saviours to their fellows and to society? Which of these two cries must it be: "On to Socialism," or "Back to Christ"? Choose between the two; it is a choice between life and death.

Remember, Socialism is a secularist ideal. It was born in secularism; it has been matured in secularism, and it remains and must continue to remain in secularism, if it is to be true to itself. Its horizon rests on the rim of this world. Were it put forward, as I have said, as a mere contribution to economics, we might not expect it to make explicit mention of a life to come, but because it is put forward, as a theory of life and as an all-embracing ideal, it must be pronounced to be a theory as dangerous as it is insidious.

Man cannot live on iced sodas and whipped cream. He needs religion, and society cannot endure without religion. Even Herbert Spencer, the modern-day philosopher, at the end of his life was forced to admit that religion is the very stuff of life, that it is necessary for all healthy and natural well-being, that it must ever be a factor in the development of a people. The fact is, as the poet puts it: "Religion is all or nothing."

An ideal, I repeat, every man must have before him. The ideal that has been before the Christian world for two thousand years is Christ.

Let Democracy rally round Him closer than ever.

As in the past He broke its chains of slavery, as in the past He proclaimed that the middle term between individualism and collectivism is divine altruism, so does He continue to preach: "Love one another as I have loved you." If there are Socialists who tell me that Christianity has already been tried and found wanting, with all the vehemence of my soul I deny it; and from this pulpit I declare before the world that it is not Christianity that has failed, but, on the contrary, it is the plentiful lack of Christianity in those calling themselves Christians which is at the root of our present anarchy and social misery and slavery. What to-day is wanted is not less but more of the Christianity which renewed the face of the earth when it was in a worse plight than it is to-day. The social organism needs to be revitalized by the Christ-Spirit.

The rivalry between Capital and Labour, if the teachings of Christ were followed, would be a rivalry of service, as in reality the true measure of Christian greatness must be interpreted in terms of service both to God and our neighbour. If only we could keep before our minds and draw into our hearts the all-embracing principles of Christ's Christianity, if only we were actuated by His motives, we should find that the solution of the economic problems before us to-day begins not with the reform of society, but with the reform of the individual.

I repeat, the greatest social Reformer the world has yet seen was Christ Himself, and it was to the individual He appealed when He came to redeem the race. His language was: "If thou wilt come after Me," "If thou wilt be perfect," "If thou wilt enter into eternal life." It was to the individual He addressed Himself; it was through the individual that He would restore fallen humanity; and it is with the individual we, too, must begin if we would associate ourselves with Him in the fruitful, if toilsome, work of Social Reformation.

Let us start this work in our own homes, and carry it forward into our own street, into our own State, till at length this Great Republic shall become renewed and revitalized with the spirit of Him who is still our Ideal, our Inspirer as well as our Redeemer.

IV

SOCIALISM AND THE FAMILY

THERE is no more beautiful creation on earth than the Christian family as it has been lived for nearly two thousand years in the well-ordered Christian home. Home! What sweet and sacred memories does that word recall to us; what hours of sunshine, peace, and joy it brings back to our lives, checkered too often by suffering and shadowed by grief! But home is a name that stands for something more than the roof tree of a family circle, it rises before us as a pillar of the State, as its strongest and noblest support.

To interfere, then, with the sanctions of married life, to attempt to shift its centre of gravity, or to dare loosen its strong human ties, means an attack upon the stability of the State itself, and is a menace to the foundation upon which it rests.

In this Conference I shall, first of all, remind you of what is the teaching of the Catholic Church with regard to marriage and the family, and I shall then go on to point out in what the teaching of Socialism differs from it. What we want

118

to discover is this: Can their views be made to agree, or are they utterly and hopelessly irreconcilable? These are questions which demand our closest attention, for we are going to test the actual foundations upon which this Great Republic depends for its stability, unity, and strength.

We know without consulting the first chapter of Genesis, or appealing to tradition, that God made the family. We infer it because the family is "the prerequisite of production, the ordinary unit of enjoyment, the foundation of national welfare and greatness, and the principal source, in the natural order, both of virtue and happiness." (C. S. Devas, "Political Economy.")

By the family I mean a compound society made up of two elementary societies, the conjugal and the parental. The former is the lasting union of a man and a woman for the purpose of propagating and educating their kind. The latter is the lasting union of parents and offspring for the purpose of education. The essential qualities of the family are thus summed up by a recent writer: —

"The object of conjugal society or marriage requires its indissolubility; the equal personal dignity of its members postulates their equality in essential rights; the nature of their union implies mutual love, friendship, and faithfulness;

the unity and harmony of action necessary for the achievement of the common end demands obedience of the wife to the husband, not like that of a slave to the master, but rather like that of a mate to a friend and of a member to the head.

"Parents are under the strict obligation, laid on them directly by the Author of nature, to impart to their children physical, intellectual, and moral education, and to devote their entire energy to the accomplishment of this task; but they are at the same time clothed with sacred and inviolable authority over them. "(Ming, "The Morality of Modern Socialism," pp. 152–153.)

What has the Catholic Church done for this natural institution, the family?

She has raised it into a higher plane. It was God-given from the beginning. The Catholic Church has made it God-like, — a picture of God. The marriage bond has become the authentic symbol of the union between Christ and His Church. It was a contract; it has become a sacrament, and a "great Sacrament." Let us go into this aspect of the question a little more fully. It will help to show how Catholic and socialist views of the family are irreconcilable.

In bridegroom and bride the Catholic Church sees not merely the prospective father and mother of a family that shall rise up to call them blessed, but generation following generation, each charged with a mission and deputed to a work for the good of Church and State.

Not without reason does St. Paul, as he contemplates the grandeur of Christian marriage, exclaim: "This is a great mystery," a mysterious religious rite, a great Sacrament. Originally a divine institution, marriage has been raised by Jesus Christ into a sacramental union.

Of all the seven sacraments, matrimony is the only one in which, not the priest, but the contracting parties themselves are the officiating ministers.

Not only does the Christian dispensation convert the natural into a religious contract, but it raises those entering into it to a sacramental state of life. Truly "It is a great sacrament." Shall we not call marriage a sublime state, giving as it does to man and wife the claims on never failing special graces to meet the special trials inevitable to their state? But the sacred career upon which man and woman enter on their wedding-day is laden with consequences, not to themselves only, but also to the State and to the Christian Church. Hence, in the midst of his eulogy of the sacrament of matrimony, the Apostle pauses to remind us that he is speaking "in Christ and in the Church."

Never, perhaps, since the letter to the Ephesians was written has there been so much reason as now, when the birth-rate is decreasing, and the divorce list is increasing, and Socialism is developing, to emphasize the warning note of the Apostle, who would seem to say, the marriage state is, indeed, sacred and sublime, nay, a mysterious rite, "a great Sacrament"; but for those only whose union in some sense symbolizes the alliance between Christ and His Church.

Regarded as a mere social contract it is shorn of all beauty and sublimity; it is a market good, often an economic asset only. For a moment let us lift the eyes of our souls to contemplate the Mystic Union referred to by St. Paul, and recognize the one supreme and absolute standard by which to gauge the rightness and sacredness of Christian wedded life.

In Christ and His Church we see a union in which three characteristics stand out in boldest prominence. It is a union which is indissolubly one; it is a union which is indefectibly true; and it is a union which is indestructibly good.

Of His Bride, the Church, Christ, the Bridegroom, says, "My perfect one is but one." So indissolubly, so intimately is she one with Him that she becomes His Body, and He her Head, so that in loving her He loves Himself; while to her He communicates His own imperishable life, declaring, with prophetic word, that no matter what the rage of kings, or the malice of men, or the gates of hell may devise for her destruction, never shall they prevail against her. The union, then, between Christ and the Church is indissoluble. But more, this Mystic Union is one that is indefectibly true; true because of the mutual trust and confidence subsisting between the divine Bridegroom and His Bride. To His Spouse, the Church, Christ, her Lord, intrusts without fear not only the proclamation of His reign, the promulgation of His laws, the teaching of His dogmatic code and the guardianship of His moral precepts, but also the custody of His reputation, of His character, nay, of His divine personality itself, knowing she will suffer neither prelate nor potentate to tamper with any the least tenet of His revealed teaching. So indefectibly true Christ knows her to be that He does not hesitate to proclaim: "He that heareth you heareth Me, and He that despiseth you despiseth Me." And so, the union between Christ and His Church is indefectible. Now let us pass from this indissoluble and indefectible character of Christ's mystic marriage with the Church to consider its indestructible goodness. It is this divine attribute of goodness, of imperishable goodness, which most of all we admire and praise in the Mystic Wedded Life to which I refer. We are told by the poet:—

'Tis only noble to be good.

How supremely true are these words! Apart from true sanctity, there is no true nobility. Not only is goodness the root, the bloom, and the fruit of nobleness, but its very beauty and its fragrance.

Whatever else she may be to those who are without spiritual insight, to the King's Son the Church is "without spot or wrinkle or any such thing"; she is holy and beautiful, "without blemish." In words such as these does the inspired Apostle eulogize the goodness and beauty of Christ's mystic Bride. This goodness, inherent in her constitution, is, like all goodness, self-diffusive, prodigal, prolific. Witness the tender piety of her little children, the patience and charitableness of her many poor, and the heroic yet attractive sympathy of her saints.

How could she well be else, seeing that to dower her with His own divine gifts Christ, her Spouse, "delivered Himself up . . . cleansing her by the laver of water in the word of life"?

Glance back down the ages and catch sight of His beloved one, at His invitation to the sacred nuptials, coming forth "as the morning rising, fair as the moon, bright as the sun, terrible as an army set in array." "This is a great Sacrament; but I speak in Christ and in the Church." The union between Christ and His Church is indestructible. Here, in the picture I have attempted to lift up before you, you may see for yourselves what are to be the chief features which man and woman who become husband and wife must copy into their own wedded life.

To nothing less than this their troth is pledged, having already at the altar said each to each, "I take thee from this day forward, for better, for worse, for richer, for poorer, in sickness and in health, till death do us part." So shall it be: —

> By your troth she shall be true,
> Ever true, as wives of yore;
> And her "Yes" once said to you,
> Shall be true for evermore.

Married life is thus indissolubly one, infallibly true, and indefectibly good — but, "I speak in Christ and in His Church."

The Catholic Church has indeed drawn closer the marriage bond, and ennobled conjugal love.

Look at the various types of the pre-Christian

family described by Mr. Devas in his "Studies of Family Life." There was much good in them, but evil had crept in with the good. The ideal family life was first revealed to the world in the cottage home at Nazareth. That example has been treasured by the Catholic Church and held up before the eyes of the world for two thousand years. No one can study the mysteries revealed to us in that homestead among the highlands of Galilee without realizing more fully what the sanctity of home life means for the Christian family.

What has been the result of this study? To answer that question would take me far beyond the limits of this Conference. But let me recall a few facts.

Christianity, and Christianity alone, has given woman her right position in the family and in society. It has honoured womanhood, wifehood, and motherhood as they had never been honoured before. Some modern writers by misunderstanding or by misinterpreting decrees of the Council of Auxerre, and the discussions at the Council of Macon, try to make out that the Catholic Church at one time doubted whether women had souls at all; and they attempt to support their thesis by citing passages from early Christian writers, notably Tertullian, Origen, and St. Jerome. But it is to no purpose. To the Catholic Church and to none other, woman must turn when she wants to point to the source of her position in Christian society. Christianity will tolerate neither the servility nor the frivolity which marks the relation of wife to husband in non-Christian civilizations. Christianity refuses to regard woman as man's drudge, or the sport of his lust. Christian marriage, as I have pointed out, is a high and holy thing, involving obligations of faithfulness and mutual honour and service which press on the husband as well as upon the wife. Christian marriage is full of responsibility and exacts a high standard, but it is rich in rewards and draws down blessings upon itself and on the country where it is held in honour.

The popular estimate of the family (writes Bishop Westcott) is "an infallible criterion of the state of society. Heroes cannot save a country where the idea of the family is degraded."

Needless to say, the Catholic Church has always stood for the sacred character of the family, nor will she have anything to do with slackening the marriage ties knit together so closely by God's own hand.

Fearlessly from this pulpit I proclaim that the Church of Christ has rendered inestimable service to civilization by insisting on the sanctity and stability of wedded life. All through the ages the Popes, no matter what the lives of some few of them may have been, have always shown themselves to be inflexible in the matter of Christian marriage. A lustful king seeks sanction from Rome for his adultery. That sanction is refused. Not by a hair's-breadth will Rome swerve, even though a king threatens to drag a great nation into schism. For no consideration, even of State, will Rome permit a reigning sovereign to dismiss his lawfully wedded wife. This fact stares out upon us Catholics, not only in the land from which I come, but I may add in all other climes also where the history of England is read. Had Pope Clement VII yielded to the pressure brought upon him by the Eighth Henry, England to-day might still have been Catholic, but the Pope refused to put asunder what God had joined together. The matter lay beyond his authority and jurisdiction.

We are living in a day when in most countries the civil law has usurped an authority beyond the powers of Christ's own Church, and has declared marriage to be not a sacred and indissoluble union, but a civil contract only — in some States of this Great Republic to be almost as easily unmade as made. This civil law of complete divorce, I need not remind you, is intrinsically wrong. It is a violation of the revealed law of God, and is condemned by the Catholic Church. There are, indeed, cases when a Catholic, who has no intention of attempting a second marriage, but is merely wanting to get civil freedom from an adulterous partner, may seek it by a sentence of divorce in the civil courts. But this is a totally distinct matter from procuring divorce with the intention of remarrying. On the question of divorce and judicial separation a Catholic holds unhesitatingly and tenaciously the teaching of the divine Master as interpreted by His Church. Accordingly, we maintain to-day, in the twentieth century, what was proclaimed in the first, that between man and wife there can be no divorce till death do them part — no divorce, that is to say, with the intention of remarrying. Behold here the wording of the Christian law. It is uncompromising, absolute, final.

If examples be cited from history which seem to show that the Holy See has known how to yield in exceptional cases, even with this divine law before its eyes, let me at once say that these examples, so freely and so often quoted, are altogether beside the mark. They are declarations of

K

nullity, not of divorce. After investigating the facts of the case submitted to it, the ecclesiastical court has come to the conclusion that the parties were never married at all; in a word, that God never joined them together. Besides, it must be borne in mind that the words of the sacred text referred to are to be understood in their rigorous sense of consummated Christian marriage only. For grave reasons the Church may dissolve a non-consummated marriage, but into this there is no time nor need, for the moment, to enter.

Outside the Church there seems to be a strong feeling against legal separation, which has been called "divorce without the right to remarry." Unquestionably, separation may be a great danger to either or both parties concerned. For that reason every influence that can be ought to be brought to stave off separation. But because such separation may be trying to virtue, it does not entitle the parties so tried to yield to temptation, to defy God's law, and at once to take proceedings for divorce with the object of remarrying. Altogether, we reject the contention that the essence of marriage is "sexual faithfulness," which, if violated by either party, begets a right for the dissolution of marriage.

We are told that England, "like other Protestant and enlightened countries," has left the Catholic Church behind to follow in this matter the United States of America. If my dear country wants to switch on and off divorce almost as easily as it does its electric light, I for one, with all the force of my being, condemn its action not only as derogatory to the best interests of the community, but still more as constructive treason against the majesty of Christ.

A modern writer has warned us that "if we want to make marriage stronger in the affections of the people we must make divorce more easily attainable." Are, then, the Catholic people of Catholic Ireland, who have no law of divorce, a melancholy and miserable community? Is it a fact that compared with Irish Catholics our Nonconformist brethren are all brightness, wit, and humour?

Truth to tell, England would do better to learn her marriage lesson from Catholic Ireland than from the United States of America. During the past forty years we have progressed rapidly enough without wishing to emulate the practices of some of the States in the great and glorious Republic of America. The rapid growth in divorce proceedings at home during the period referred to ought in all conscience to satisfy the wildest advocates of divorce. My experience of the working classes, confined not altogether to the Catholic community, does not lead me to think that they feel very much aggrieved by the law as it at present stands. Quarrels between man and wife are more readily adjusted among them than they are in classes higher up the social ladder. They settle their own differences without extraneous aid. They accept the inevitable; as a rule, they forgive and forget. Is the commercial instinct so highly developed in some of us that we at once consider it part of our mission, where there is no want of divorce, to create it? What England, with most other lands to-day, needs, is not what must tend, by breaking up the family, to disintegrate her Empire, but on the contrary, what most of all she desiderates is what knits into closer intimacy the ties of family, that so the country may grow for her a race of sons, pure, brave, and strong to hold their own against the world. "Divorce made easy," "done while you wait," will not make for the manliness of any race. There is nothing in it with which to stiffen and strengthen character. Divorce, with rare exception, spells betrayal of troth, surrender of principle, national disaster.

And now let me pass to speak of the offspring of married life. The Church rejects the old pagan view that the child is merely the property of the parents; she holds that the child has received its immortal soul directly from God. Yet she also rejects the false philosophy which would sever the child from its parents, and make it the property of the State. Parents and children are closely knit together by links of mutual duty and love, with which no State may interfere. Again and again has the Catholic Church had to protest against governments, which, blindly ignorant of the true sources of national strength and well-being, have endeavoured to weaken family ties and assume the duties which properly belong to parentage. The one, unchanging Catholic cry through the past three decades of years has been the plea for parental rights in determining what shall be the child's religious education. Upon this question the Catholic Church has made herself heard and felt as none other. Pope Leo in his Encyclical on the "Condition of Labor," says: "Parental authority can be neither abolished nor absorbed by the State; for it has the same source as human life itself. The child belongs to the father, and is, as it were, the continuation of the father's personality; and, speaking strictly, the child takes its place in civil society not by its own right, but in its quality as a member of the family in which it is born. And for the very reason that 'the child belongs to the father,' it is, as St. Thomas of Aquin says, 'before it attains the use of free-will, under power and charge of its parents.' The Socialists, therefore, in setting aside the parent and setting up a State supervision, act against natural justice, and break into pieces the stability of the family."

"Every child," says Bebel, "that comes into the world, whether male or female, is a welcome addition to society; for society beholds in every child the continuation of itself and its own further development; it therefore perceives from the very outset the duty, according to its power, to provide for the new-born child." The children must, therefore, be taken at the earliest possible age into the care of the State, and this is the Socialist's ideal. All means of education and instruction, even clothing and food, will be supplied by the State. The Erfurt platform demands: "Secularization of the schools. Compulsory attendance at the public schools. Instruction, use of all means of instruction, and board free of charge in all public elementary schools and in the higher institutions of learning for such pupils of both sexes as, on account of their talents, are judged fit for higher studies." The American

Socialist Party platform adopted in Chicago, 1904, advocates, "education of all children up to the age of eighteen years, and State and municipal aid for books, clothing, and food."

What does the Socialist propose to teach the young American? Loyalty to country, patriotism? Not so. Peruse the Socialist Primer by Nicholas Klein, and sold and distributed in tens of thousands, and ask yourselves what type of citizen does Socialism undertake to train and educate. I will here reproduce one lesson out of the many in this primer.

LESSON XXIV

Here is a man with a gun; he is in the troop. You see he has a nice suit on. Does he work? No, the man with the gun does no work. His work is to shoot men who do work.

Is it nice to shoot men? Would you like to shoot a man?

This man eats, drinks, wears clothes, but he does no work. Do you think that this is nice? Yes, this is nice for the Fat Man, but bad for the Thin, so he owns the man with the gun. When the Thin man will have the law on his side, there will be no more men with guns.

Who makes the gun? The man who works.

Who makes the nice suit? The man who works.

Who gets shot with the gun? The man who works.

Who gets the bad clothes? The man who works.

Is this right? No, this is wrong!

The man who works should have good clothes, and all that is good.

The man with the gun must go to work, too.

War must come to an end. War is bad. Peace is good.

Surely, if this is the doctrine of Socialism, and nobody can doubt it, then C. S. Devas is right when he says: "The sacred union of man and woman for mutual help, for educating and supporting their children, for providing for their future welfare, the sense of mutual responsibility and care, the true and healthy communism, that of the home, the countless coöperative associations which each family forms, the thousand ties of dependence that are occasion for the display of the best qualities of human nature — this realm of self-devotion and self-sacrifice — all this becomes unmeaning and impossible where the socialist State provides for the nourishment and education and technical training and material and moral outfit of each child. The moral office of parents is gone, the sacred enclosure of home is violated, the sacred words father, mother, sister, have been degraded to a lower meaning, and the next step is to reduce the rearing of man under approved physicians and physiologists and the latest professors of eugenics, to the level of a prize-cattle farm. The Christian family and Collectivism are incompatible; their antagonism is so rooted that reconciliation is impossible."

Marriage, let me repeat, is a divine institution, raised by the Founder of Christianity to the dignity of a Sacrament. Catholics who enter this sacramental state of life should do so only after serious and sacred thought, and when strong in their resolve, come what may, to remain faithful each to each not till fondness, but till death, do them part.

If only husbands and wives were a little less exacting, if only they made more allowance for their differences in tastes and in heredity, in temperament and in character, if instead of expecting so much more they were to be contented with far less each from each; if, in a word, their demands upon one another's lives instead of being measured by what each wanted from the other were to be regulated by what the other could give, then in the words of the poet, after years of happy wedded life to the wife's whisper,

"More years have made me love thee more,"

there would be heard the husband's firm reply,

"There is none I love like thee."

I shall perhaps be reminded by some Socialist that Catholic family life is not without its failures, that instances numerous enough might be cited to show that there have been, and are, not a few serious breakdowns in the homes of families calling themselves Catholic.

Alas! to my disappointment and shame, I know it only too well. But a thousand instances of infidelity, coupled, if you will, with cruelty, do not go to prove that the Christian family, as such, is a failure.

If you insist on reminding me of the failures, I must tell you of the causes that have led up to them. The Church is not to be blamed for these lapses, for these broken vows. It is not her mission to coerce man and wife; she could not, even if she would, change them into automatic machinery. She knows human nature far too intimately to rely upon any such mechanical process for regulating life. She will remind you that it is not the Christian family, loyal and true to her, but the family fallen away from her teaching, that has failed. The family that has sold its birthright, the family that has betrayed its spiritual mother, the family that has forgotten its Christian origin, — that is the family which is the failure. And it is a failure because of its lapse from Catholic teachers and Catholic principle and practice.

The French Socialist Le Pay and his school have established beyond dispute the fact that the Christian ideal of the family, as set up by the Church, is still in our own time a potent influence for good. Where Christianity is strong there, he reminds us, family life too is strong. "Who," for example, asks a modern writer, "has not heard of Ireland and how there a vast population have in virtue of their religion and by docility to its teaching shown a shining example of Christian family life, sins of the flesh scarcely being known among them, and reverence for parents and dutiful care of their brethren being universal."

May God bless Ireland and its brave sons

and pure daughters for the example they have set in this matter to the rest of the Christian world.

But it is not in Catholic Ireland alone that the Christian family is to be found in all its vigour, love, and beauty. In every land and in every section of a Christian community, if you have eyes to see, you will discover lofty and holy examples of Catholic home life and home practices. How often have I not heard both from those high up and those low down the social ladder exclamations such as this: "Whatever good there is in me I owe to my home." Nay, when all else has failed to appeal to the heartless heart of some prodigal, the mere mention of the word "home" oftener than not will touch some hidden spring in his soul, and he will sink to his knees broken and contrite.

It is a gross and mischievous exaggeration, therefore, to say, as many Socialists say, that the Christian family has proved a failure. Mr. Wells tells us (" New Worlds for Old," p. 125) that he has "very grave doubts if the world has ever yet held a high percentage of good homes." I do not imply for an instant that Mr. Wells seeks to destroy the family. On the contrary, he seeks to raise it to a higher level. But I do not think that he understands the sound elements of family life that are to be found amongst us, and which we must make use of if we are to effect a sound and lasting social reform.

Now I agree entirely with Mr. Wells that modern conditions of life, especially in our great cities, are seriously prejudicial to the integrity of family life; so prejudicial as to constitute a disgrace to our civilization. No one who has worked among the poor can fail to be moved by the appalling waste of human life, the misery and squalor, the dirt and the disease, the absence of all that can be called home for many of our brothers and sisters. The spectacle is truly appalling, and every man and woman, with a particle of human sympathy in their constitution, must absolutely lend their aid in remedying this hideous condition of affairs.

It is not surprising that people should grow impatient of palliatives before the spectacle of such deep-rooted misery. It is not astonishing that they should welcome Socialism, which claims to be the only means of setting right such a colossal wrong. But the Catholic Church, with her experience so wide and vast and long, precisely because she loves the poor will not countenance Socialism. She will not countenance it because she knows, better than any man or any body of men, how human nature may be built up, how the truest welfare of a people may be secured. She knows the toiling poor better than any compiler of blue books can know them. She knows that the regeneration of the Christian family by the Christian spirit must be the basis of sound social reform. And she knows that Socialism, despite the disclaimers and good intentions of some of its adherents, does really constitute an attack on the Christian family. There is nothing in common between the Socialism and the Catholic household.

Divorce is bad enough, race suicide is worse. We read in "Social Adjustment," p. 153, that "instead of the 100,000,000 descendants of native-born population in the States predicted for 1900, there were but 41,000,000 in existence. The advent of the other 59,000,000 was prevented by a conscious restriction of the birth-rate." To the question put by Democracy: "How can I rise, like the man with the plug-hat?" came the answer of the socialist economist, "Stop having children." "The advice," Professor Scott answers triumphantly, "was followed. The family of eight is replaced by the family of two, and thus the labourer is enabled to raise his standard of life." The professor continues (pp. 159, 160): "In all groups of modern society the size of the family is being restricted, because of the demand for quality, rather than quantity, of children." Again, "The amount of income should determine the number of children."

Once more: "Wages must eventually be raised; but while they retain their present relation to prices the average family can afford no more than three children. In every trade men and women are recognizing this fact, and restricting the size of their families accordingly." This iniquitous, criminal state of things from the Christian point of view, the professor of Wharton School regards as "a great step forward." He thinks it will guarantee, first, that no child will be brought into the world who cannot be properly cared for, and secondly, that all children brought into life will live joyous and useful lives.

Alas! "not on bread alone doth man live." Christians recognize that lives "joyous" and "useful" can never be wrung out of practices which convert married life into a state of legal prostitution.

Let me again remind you that one main reason of the Church's condemnation of Socialism is that it proposes to reorganize, or rather to disorganize, the Christian home as we have known it all these ages. Socialism, if we study it ethically, we shall find to be committed to a set of ideas about wedded life and home which I am forced to describe as not only foreign, but as repulsive to all of us who have been trained in the Old Tradition, in the School of Christ.

The Socialist, who is something more than a mere social reformer, cannot well avoid attacking the institution of the family as we know it. It is bred in him to do so, because it is an essential constituent of historical Socialism. This, I shall proceed to show, is no gratuitous assertion; it is borne out by a "cloud of witnesses." Take the book called "The Origin of the Family," and referred to by Socialists as "an intellectual treat," a "great socialist classic." In this work we are assured that "monogamy was not founded on nature, but on economic considerations; namely, the victory of private property over primitive and natural collectivism." The author informs us that under Socialism marriage will no longer be indissoluble. He informs us that marriage is moral only so long as love lasts. "The duration," he writes, "of an attack of individual sex-love varies considerably according to individual disposition, especially in men. A positive cessation of fondness, or its replacement by a new passionate love, makes a separation a blessing for both parties, and society." No passage in that socialist "classic" can, I venture to say, be made to fit in with the gospel of Christianity. Again, take the Socialist's international text-book on the woman question. "Woman" has run through more than fifty editions in Germany alone. In it are passages such as this: "The satisfaction of the sexual impulse is as much a private concern of each individual as the satisfaction of any other natural impulse. No one is accountable to any one else, and no third person has a right to interfere. . . . If between man and woman who have entered into a union incompatibility, disappointment, or revulsion should appear, morality commands a dissolution of the union which has become unnatural, and therefore immoral." This "socialist classic," full of passages such as I have cited, differs in every line from the Gospel of Christ, as all the world can see. Once more, in a work written by "the greatest man the socialist movement has yet claimed in England " and entitled "Socialism, Its Growth and Outcome," we read that under a socialistic régime "property in children would cease to exist, and every infant that came into the world would be born into full

L

citizenship and would enjoy all its advantages, whatever the conduct of its parents might be. Thus a new development of the family would take place on the basis, not of a predetermined, lifelong business arrangement, to be formally and nominally held to, irrespective of circumstances, but on mental inclination and affection, an association terminable at the will of either party." This teaching requires no comment from me. Lastly, we are told in "Socialism — Positive and Negative," a work described as "brilliant, fearless, searching," that "socialist parties do not attack Religion, the Family, and the State," but the "brilliant author" makes a point of reminding us that "Socialist Philosophy proves conclusively that the legislation of the positive political and economic ideals of Socialism involves the atrophy of Religion, the metamorphosis of the Family, and the suicide of the State," as we understand it. This quotation speaks for itself. My implacable quarrel, then, with Socialism is this — that in its recognized classics, in its propaganda, in its press, and in its unguarded utterances, it propounds and proclaims a gospel about wedded and family life altogether subversive of the teaching of Christianity. No sane man can give himself up to the study of Socialism without coming to the conclusion that, taken as an ethical and as an economic theory of life, it is committed to doctrines about marriage which it would seem must inevitably destroy the home, and so undermine the State. Socialism is founded on a philosophy of life which makes the indissolubility of marriage ridiculous, which makes race suicide rational, and makes children the property of the State.

Needless to say, I shall be told by individual Socialists that I have entirely misrepresented the Socialist's position with regard to marriage, its rights and its duties. In answer to this charge let me say that I have uttered nothing but what I have drawn from their own very much read and very highly recommended socialist classics. Those works have not been withdrawn. They are still being poured forth every day by the socialist press.

Now, I do not wish to do any one an injustice. I know full well that there are quite a number of Socialists who repudiate the doctrine I have enunciated, and have publicly acknowledged the necessity for maintaining the Christian ideal of the family. What do they prove? They prove, at most, that a number of people calling themselves Socialists believe that Socialism would not prejudice the family. I am ready to give them credit for being perfectly sincere in believing this, but I am not prepared to believe it myself, for the evidence is against them. With regard to this matter, let me observe, in the first place, these writers who claim that Socialism will not prejudice the family can speak only for themselves. They can only mean that they do not desire to see the Christian family broken up. They cannot speak for Socialism as a whole. They cannot bind their fellow-Socialists, for, notice well, Socialism, unlike the Catholic Church, has no living and binding authoritative voice. It is a conglomeration of opinions, of sentiments, of activities, clustering around an economic proposal, an illegal scheme. True, there are groups and parties and schools, but none of them has any right to say to the others: "You are not Socialists. I oppose your views." On the contrary, if I, as a Catholic priest, say the Catholic Church forbids polygamy, and you ask me for my authority, I have an authority to which I can turn and make appeal. That authority will come down heavily with pains and penalties on me or any other Catholic priest or prelate who would venture, would dare, to advocate polygamy or free love union. But what authority can Wells or Mac-

Donald and Company invoke in order to make their fellow-Socialists accept their championship of the family? The Socialist brought up on Bax will claim to be quite as good a Socialist as Wells, and the followers of Morris will not listen to MacDonald, and in the event of a socialist régime they will endeavour to secure such legislation on the subject as accords with their own individual views. No one needs to doubt whose views in the long run would prevail. Let there be no mistake about it. It is the family, as interpreted by Christianity, which actually stands in the way of Socialism, and until the Christian family is disposed of, Socialism realizes that it can make no headway. Like the National Convention in Paris, Socialism to-day sees no hope of running up its red flag and of keeping it flying so long as family life eludes its death grip. Until the Christian marriage becomes changed into a civil contract, and children become State property, Socialism cannot have a free hand, cannot run down the Stars and Stripes floating over the White House.

Socialists, instead of finding fault with me for quoting from their own recognized authorities, would do well first of all to issue an expurgated edition of their classics, or else to withdraw them once and for all from the book market, repudiating as unsocialistic the teachings which they unfold and propound. Until Socialism shall have shifted its centre of gravity from anti-Christian premises, until Socialists shall have publicly renounced the philosophy of life as formulated by the founders of their cult, and until their men of light and leading shall have made it clear to us that Socialism indorses, upholds, and enforces the time-honored traditions of the Christian family and the Christian home, we have no alternative but to denounce Socialism from pulpit and platform, in public and private, as a most insidious menace to the State which must rest on its own God-given foundation, the Home.

I have done. My one request to you before I leave the pulpit is that you will steadily bear in mind that, if Socialism meant nothing more than an economic system, transferring to the State all railways, telegraphs, highroads, gas plants, fire brigades, and such like ventures and enterprises, the Church neither would want nor ought to interfere. Socialism would then be no business of hers. She would hold her peace. Why, then, does she stand up and raise her voice denouncing and condemning Socialism as a menace to the family?

She does so because she sees that Socialism, no matter what it may propose in theory, in practice attempts to invade the home, to loosen wedded ties, to usurp parental rights, proclaiming to man and wife that their plighted troth to be in riches and in poverty, in sickness and in health, loyal each to each, has a civil binding force only, and that the tie between them is not indissoluble. The Catholic Church, as the Guardian of Faith, and as the accredited Teacher of the Gospel of Christ, would be untrue to her divine mission, if after studying the ethics of marriage as propounded and propagated through the socialist schools of philosophy, she did not express her mind about its teachings and its tendencies. She has done so in language about which there can be no mistake. Sovereign pontiffs have declared that till Socialism clears itself of the charge of unorthodoxy in its doctrine and philosophy about married life and home duties, no true son of the Church may identify himself with Socialism.

In his Encyclical dealing with this subject, Pope Leo XIII, after reminding the faithful that "the governing principle of family life has, in accordance with the requirements of natural law, its basis in the indissoluble union of husband and wife, and its superstructure in the duties and rights of parents and children," goes on to drive home these weighty words of warning which I now repeat to you. "You are aware," writes His Holiness, "that the theories of Socialism would quickly destroy this family life, since the stability afforded by marriage under religious sanction once lost, parental authority over children and duties of children to parents are necessarily and most harmfully slackened. Socialists," the Pope declares, "in setting aside the parent and setting up a State supervision, act against natural justice and break into pieces the stability of all family life."

No philosophy of life which is in contradiction with the natural law, and which breaks into pieces the stability of the family can be made, by any possible mental process, to fit in with the tenets of Christianity. "But," insists the Holy Father, "this is the teaching of Socialism," and therefore to accept the philosophy of Socialism is to reject the teaching of the Church. The two Schools hold views about marriage ties and home duties as opposite to each other as North to South. They are poles apart. And all hope of bringing them together vanishes from my mind like a dream.

V

SOCIALISM AND RELIGION

NOT many weeks ago I was strolling across a common on the outskirts of an eastern state city, when I found myself drawn to the fringe of a closely packed throng of men, who, with keenest relish, were gulping down a very torrent of invective that was being poured upon them by a tall, gaunt figure standing on a platform in their midst. "It is a libel, comrades," exclaimed the orator; "we are not rough on rats upon religion. Let them that wants it have it, as for us it is not the churches we are after, but the land. We have no use for any clap-trap mountain-gospel, with its blessings on those who invite the capitalist to smite them on both cheeks; nor do we believe in a beatitude which promises heaven to any craven spirit who meekly grinds himself to death for a starvation wage in a sweatshop. We have done with all such stagnant religion. Our mission is to create wants in the people and to force capitalists to supply them. That is my religion, and that is yours."

I find street-corner Socialism in all countries the same. What I hear in the States, I have heard in Canada, I have heard in France, in Belgium, in Italy, and in England.

To-day we want to examine dispassionately but unsparingly the socialist attitude towards religion. What value does the Socialism which is alive in the street and in the press set upon religion? How does it regard morality and religion, those pillars of the State, "those buttresses," as Washington called them, "of human life"? I am not here asking whether Socialism as a mere economic theory is bound up with religion or irreligion, but I am asking whether the socialist movement in the concrete, as a going concern, "as a philosophy of human progress, as a theory of social evolution, as an ethical practice," is or is not an irreligious movement, and in particular is or is not a movement hostile to Christianity.

To estimate it aright, we must judge it as a whole. We must take a general view of its tendencies, of its spirit, of its so-called ideals, its aims and ambitions; we must by no means do it the injustice of mistaking the personal opinions of its members for the spirit generated in its inception by the movement itself, and inextricably bound up with it.

If, then, you ask me what is the spirit that from first to last has characterized the living, energizing thing known to us as Socialism, I have no hesitation in answering that it is a spirit as antagonistic to Christianity as darkness is to light. Read the deliberate utterances of its founders and of its leaders in every land, and at every stage of its progress, and you can come to no other conclusion than that the pioneers, philosophers, and representatives of thorough-going Socialism have proclaimed that between Socialism and Religion no banns can be published, no alliance can be recognized, no union can occur.

Let us begin with Karl Marx, the man who, according to Ramsay MacDonald, taught Socialism its own real meaning, translated its feelings into a dogma, and discovered its legitimate genesis. No doubt, I shall be told by some Socialists that Marx counts as a "back-number," that he and his doctrine are dead and gone. That is not true. Marx and Engels are still classical, even here in the New World. The authority and influence of Marx remains to-day undimmed and undiminished. The victory of the Marxists at the Amsterdam Congress gives the lie to the mild utterances of my objectors.

We are then concerned to know how did Marx

and his associates regard the relations of Socialism
to Christianity. We are told by so respectable an
authority as H. G. Wells that the Socialism of
Marx and Engels was "strongly anti-Christian in
tone." Observe well that he does not state that
these men themselves, apart from their Socialism,
were anti-Christian in tone, but Wells is at pains
to remind us that their hostility to Christianity
was bound up with their Socialism; that in the
measure in which they were Socialists they were
antagonistic to Christianity.

And, indeed, how could it be otherwise, seeing
that Socialism is historically based upon a conception of the Universe which leaves no room for
religion? It is built up upon materialism, and
thoroughgoing Socialists are proud of its origin,
and are trying everywhere to inculcate its materialistic principles.

"It is incontrovertible," says Bernstein, "that
the most important part in the foundation of
Marxism is its specific theory of history which
goes by the name of the materialistic conception of history. It was the boast of Marx that
Socialism would deliver men's conscience from
what he called the 'spectre of religion.'" John
Spargo says: "The founders of modern scientific Socialism took the dogmas of Christianity

at that time and held them up to intellectual scorn — a task by no means arduous." (Spargo, "Spiritual Significance of Modern Socialism," p. 86.)

In fact, when we look to the genesis of Socialism, we find that it first takes shape not merely as an economic method of curing the abuses of Capitalism, but as a new way of life, a shifting of all man's hopes and aspirations. It is, in fact, offered to the world as a substitute for religion. Nay, it cannot even find a basis on which to stand except on the ruins of Christianity, whose place it hopes fully to occupy, whose mission it promises more than to fulfil.

Marx declared that the abolition of religion was a necessary condition for the true happiness of the people. (*Volksblatt*, No. 281.) In his criticism of the socialist platform he calls upon the labour party to declare its intention "of delivering men's consciences from the spectre of religion" (p. 564).

" In what sense Socialism is not religion," writes Balfort Bax (" Socialism and Religion "), " is clear. It utterly despises the 'other world' with all its stage properties . . . . The Socialist whose 'social creed' is his only religion requires no travesty of Christian rites to aid him in keeping his ideal before him."

"We have simply done with God," cries Marx's henchman, Engels. "We must face and wipe out," shouts another, "those two curses, the curses of Capitalism and Christianity. Until that is done, nothing can be done," avows Dr. Aveling, the "free" husband of Marx's daughter.

I will not weary you by a multiplication of quotations. Peruse socialistic literature, study its so-called classics, and you will arrive at one conclusion only, that between Socialism and revealed religion there can be no possible *modus vivendi*.

Individual Socialists will rise up, exclaiming: "Nous avons changé tout cela." Let them protest; they do not count. The men who count in this movement are men like Bebel, "one of the greatest powers of Europe," Mr. Hunter calls him. If you ask this leading Socialist how Christianity and Socialism are corelated, he will answer clearly and definitely that "Christianity and Socialism stand toward each other as fire and water." I want you to observe that Bebel is not here professing only his own disbelief in Christianity; on the contrary, he is here speaking on behalf of Socialism itself, and he publicly proclaims that Socialism in its nature and essence is opposed to Christianity as fire is to water. If I mistake not, in the Reichstag he went further, declaring before the assembled House that in religion Socialists profess atheism.

Is Bebel alone? Does he stand out in splendid isolation from his fellows? No. Liebknecht, whose influence is only little short of Bebel's, has proclaimed from the housetops that the duty of Socialists as Socialists is to root out faith in God, or, to borrow his own language, he tells the world that no one is worthy of the name of Socialist who does not consecrate himself to the spread of atheism.

Schäffle has reminded us that Social Democracy has *ex-cathedra* avowed atheism to be its religion. I might continue quotations, citing leading Socialists on both sides of the Atlantic, proving up to the hilt that the Socialism, which is not busying itself with undermining the very foundations of all belief in revealed religion and a personal God, is only a diluted Socialism, a Socialism offered to novices. It is not the genuine thing, and has no right to the brand labelled "Genuine Socialism." I shall be told, of course, that the more modern Socialism has cleared itself of its anti-Christian tendencies, that it stands neither for nor against religious principles. In answer to these assertions let me refer to a passage from "The Comrade," New York, 1903 : —

"How often do we see quoted in our own press

that familiar fallacy that 'the ethics of Christianity and Socialism are identical.' It is not true. We do not ourselves, in most cases, believe it. We repeat it because it appeals to the slave-mind of the world .... Socialism as an ethical interpretation of life is far removed from Christianity, and is of infinitely greater beauty and worth."

Let us turn to Ferri, a leading Italian Socialist, to whose indefatigable propaganda is due much of the socialist organization among the peasants of Italy. "In common with most Marxian Socialists," writes Mr. Ramsay Macdonald, "Ferri attacks religion and capitalism, marriage (as we know it) and private property in the means of production in the same breath." These words occur in the preface to a translation of a work of Ferri's, published by the Independent Labour Party with no repudiation of his blasphemies from which we take the following sentences : —

"Socialism . . . tends to substitute itself for religion. . . . It knows that the absence or lessening of the belief in God is one of the most powerful factors in its extension." ("Socialism and Positive Science," p. 49.)

Similar utterances might be quoted from the writings and speeches of the leading Socialists of Europe and America.

The anti-Christian spirit of Socialism, taking the movement as a whole, has also been pointed out by historical and scientific students of the subject both within and without the socialist camp.

Thus Professor Karl Pearson, a leading English socialist philosopher, writes as follows : —

"Socialism is based upon a conception of morality differing *in toto* from the current Christian ideal, which it does not hesitate to call anti-social and immoral. . . . The modern socialist theory of morality is based upon the agnostic treatment of the supra-sensuous . . . Can a greater gulf be imagined than really exists between current Christianity and the socialistic code ?" (" The Ethic of Free Thought," pp. 318, 319.)

"Modern Socialism," wrote Henry George, "is without religion, and its tendency is atheistic." (" Science of Political Economy," p. 198.)

"Socialism of the present day," says Professor Schaeffel, "is thoroughly irreligious and hostile to the Church. It says that the Church is only a police institution for upholding Capital, and that it deceives the common people with a 'check payable in heaven' that the Church deserves to perish." (" Quintessence of Socialism," p. 116.)

The Berlin *Vorwarts* reminds its readers that we believe in no Redeemer, but we believe in re-

M

demption. No man, no God in human form, no Saviour, can redeem humanity. Only humanity itself, only labouring humanity, can save humanity.

For Pentecost, 1893, the same paper informed its readers that "Socialism is a new doctrine and proclaims the joyful gospel of redemption, but not of redemption through a Messias."

The *New York Volkszeitung* speaks much on the same lines : "We do not believe," it writes, "in the Saviour of the Christians. Our saviour will come in the shape of the world-redeeming principle of Socialism." (Quoted by Cathrein, "Socialism," p. 221.) Blatchford is at pains to tell us : "That the whole of this old Christian doctrine is a mass of error. There was no Creator. There was no Fall. There was no Atonement." ("God and My Neighbor," p. 125.) In the *Vorwarts*, 1901, Bebel does not hesitate to say : "Christianity is the enemy of liberty and civilization. It has kept mankind in slavery and oppression." "Christianity and tyranny," according to the teaching of the "Comrade" (New York, 1903), "are, and for ages have been, firmly allied. . . . There is no wrong which has not been justified by Christianity. Its very basis is a lie, and a denial of the basic principle of Socialism." Again, of Christianity, G. S. Herrons, who is, or was, representative of

American Socialism in the International Bureau, says: "It is a huge and ghastly parasite. . . . The spiritual deliverance of the race depends on its escape from the parasite." Once more Bax contends that: "It is useless blinking the fact that this Christian doctrine is more revolting to the higher moral sense of to-day than the Saturnalia, or the cult of Proserpine could have been to the conscience of the early Christians." ("Ethics of Socialism," p. 250.) The *Sozial Demokrat* sums up the situation by saying: "Christianity is the greatest enemy of Socialism. When God is expelled from human brains, what is called Divine Grace will at the same time be banished; and when the heaven above appears nothing more than an immense falsehood, men will seek to create for themselves a heaven below." (It will be a second Babel.)

So you see if we turn from the acknowledged leaders and students of Socialism, we find the anti-Christian spirit rampant. We find resolutions passed, threatening with expulsion any comrade who supports positive religion (Madrid, September, 1892), and declaring Socialism to be directly contradictory to the immutable dogmas of the Catholic Church. "Christianity," says the *Sozial Demokrat*, the official organ of the German

Socialist, "is the bitterest foe of the Social Democracy" (May 25, 1880).

Of the blasphemous parodies of the most sacred Christian institutions to be found in such socialist papers as the Berlin *Vorwarts* (circulation 120,000) or the *Wahre Jakob* (circulation 230,000) or the Italian *Asino*, I need not speak. They are beyond measure revolting. Yet they are no mere exhibitions of personal anti-religious prejudice. They are put forward in the name of Socialism, and we find them encouraged and supported by socialist leaders. There is no getting away from the fact that Socialism as a going concern is essentially anti-Christian.

Let me repeat it: I am not asking whether Socialism, as a bare economic theory, is or is not incompatible with Christianity; nor am I asking whether individual Socialists are or are not anti-Christian: I am asking whether the actual movement called Socialism is or is not deeply imbued with an essentially anti-Christian spirit. The above instances are but a few out of a host which might be cited. But they may suffice for our purpose. It is impossible in a single Conference to cite as many witnesses as I should like.

It would seem, then, to be no mere accident that gives this materialistic colour to the products of socialistic platform and press. Hostility to Christianity is no sporadic growth in Socialism. It is, as I have said, of the very stuff and substance of the actual movement. For Socialism presents itself to us throughout its course, not merely as an economic system to be adopted on its merits and subordinated to higher ideals, but as a new way of life, readjusting our beliefs in every direction. It claims and has ever claimed to fill the entire canvas of life, to absorb all man's energies, to serve not merely as partial means, but as his entire end. Socialism would dominate every department of human activity. Socialists will not tolerate the organized religion founded by Christ. Nor is there any wide difference in this respect between the old Socialism and the new. What Marx and Engels bluntly declare, Bebel and Liebknecht, Ferri and Guesde, as bluntly reiterate — that they have done with Christianity.

Yet Mr. H. G. Wells persists in thinking that the Catholic Church has fallen into the stupid mistake of confusing the private anti-religious utterances of particular Socialists with the socialist movement itself. He speaks of the "lamentable association of two entirely separate thought processes, one constructive socially and the other destructive intellectually." ("New Worlds for Old,"

p. 198.) Similarly Mr. Bruce Glasier, the editor of the *Labour Leader*, has been triumphantly citing the cases of Liberals and Tories who have been irreligious or immoral. Such people are found in the ranks of every association, he urges. Why, then, saddle Socialism with their anti-religious or immoral words and actions?

The Catholic Church has made no such foolish mistake as is here attributed to her. She has not taken the measure of Socialism from speeches and conduct for which Socialism is not responsible, any more than she has taken the measure of Socialism from the suggestive and entertaining volumes of Mr. Wells, or the valuable economic writings of Mr. Webb. She does not judge of the movement by what Mr. Belfort Bax says any more than she judges of it by what Mr. Stewart Headlam says. She measures the movement in its entirety, noting its essential features, observing its basic suppositions, investigating its inner spirit. She estimates how far its hostility to Christianity proceeds from its very constitution and how far it is due to "an entirely separate thought process." And she declares without passion, but without hesitation, that the actual movement called Socialism is prejudicial to man's spiritual welfare, and that the danger has not ceased to exist even though the blunt anti-Christian utterances of the more outspoken have in some quarters been modified to an assurance that to Socialism "religion is a private concern." What that assurance is worth Father Joseph Husslein has proved. (See his last work, "Socialism and Social Problems.")

I read only the other day in a leading magazine that the "old Religion being vitally connected with the old morality, men have distinctly broken with it altogether; that the only ethics worth considering are the ethics which lay stress on social reform, and that Christianity no more fits our times than snow-storms fit the heat of summer."

In his "Socialism in Theory and Practice" Hillquit says: "Without fear of serious contradiction we may define ethics as the science or art of 'right' individual conduct of men towards their fellowmen." After reviewing Theological, Juridical, Intuitional, Idealist, Utilitarian doctrines on the subject of ethics, of right and wrong, Morris Hillquit goes on to offer his socialist views of the "Evolution of the Moral Sense," and he arrives at the conviction that: "The moral sense is a product of the process of evolution of man, gained in his early struggle for existence, precisely in the same manner as his intellectual qualities. It is a property of man in a state of society just as much as any of his physical organs, or as Mr. Bax puts it, 'the ethical sentiment is the correlate in the ideal sphere, of the fact of social existence itself in the material sphere.' The one is necessarily implied in the other, as the man is implied in his shadow."

He goes on to ask: "What, then, is the true standard of morality applicable to modern society?"

He proceeds to cite La Monte ("Socialism, Positive and Negative," Chicago, 1907, pp. 60, 61), and writes:—

"'Ethics,' says Mr. La Monte rather forcibly, 'simply registers the decrees by which the ruling class stamps with approval or brands with censure human conduct solely with reference to the effect of that conduct on the welfare of their class. This does not mean that any ruling class has ever had the wit to devise *ab initio* a code of ethics perfectly adapted to further their interests. Far from it. The process has seldom, if ever, been a conscious one. By a process akin to natural selection in the organic world, the ruling class learns by experience what conduct is helpful and what hurtful to it, and blesses in the one case and damns in the other. And as the ruling class has always controlled all the avenues by which ideas reach the so-called lower classes, they have heretofore been able to impose upon the subject classes just those morals which were best adapted to prolong their subjection.'"

Again, a little further on, Hillquit says: "The struggles between the bourgeoisie, the progenitors of the modern capitalist class, and the ruling class of landowners, have yielded many valuable acquisitions to modern civilization, and have resulted in the establishment of modern society, which with all its faults and imperfections is vastly superior to the feudal order which it displaced. The struggles of the dependent classes against the ruling classes in modern society have already produced the rudiments of a nobler social morality, and are rapidly preparing the ground for a still higher order of civilization.

"The modern working class is gradually but rapidly emancipating itself from the special morality of the ruling classes. In their common struggles against the oppression of the capitalist class the workers are naturally led to the recognition of the value of compact organization and solidary, harmonious action. Within their own ranks they have no motive for struggle or competition; their interests are in the opposite direction. And as the struggles of their class against the rule of capitalism become more general and concrete, more conscious and effective, there grows in them a sentiment of class loyalty, class solidarity, and class consciousness which is the basis of a new and distinct code of ethics. The modern labour movement is maturing its own standards of right and wrong conduct, its own social ideals and morality. Good or bad conduct has largely come to mean to them conduct conducive to the welfare and success of their class in its struggles for emancipation. They admire the true, militant, and devoted 'labour leader,' the hero in their struggles against the employing class. They detest the 'scab,' the deserter from their ranks in these struggles."

Here, for a moment, let me draw your attention to some extracts from "Socialism v. Religion," which tell us how the comrade class detests religion no less.

" As part of the essential educational work that must be done before this emancipation can be achieved the present pamphlet has its place. It is an entirely proletarian product, and treats a serious subject seriously and scientifically. It is issued, not as the view of an individual, but as the accepted manifesto of the Socialist Party on the subject; and agreement with it and the general position of the Party entails upon every member of the working class the duty of joining the Socialist Party of Great Britain and helping forward its work."—THE EXECUTIVE COMMITTEE OF THE SOCIALIST PARTY OF GREAT BRITAIN. *January, 1911.*

In this official pamphlet the question at the outset is asked:—

"Is Socialism antagonistic to religion? Can a Socialist be a Christian?" and then it goes on to say that "an explanation of the Socialist position on this question is the more urgent now, because the hypocritical and time-serving procedure of so many professed Socialists has enabled those who are frankly our opponents to keep the anti-religious aspect of Socialism effectively to the fore. Politicians angling for votes and office, and organizations scheming for members and subscriptions, have almost all evaded the charge that Socialism implies atheism and materialism, by pretending that religion is in no way related to the question of Socialism."

According to the teaching of S. P. G. B., religion is the outcome of social ideas and economic conditions. We are told that "God did not create man, man created God in his own image."

Contrary to all reading of history the Socialist Party of Great Britain would have us believe that "Christianity, indeed, is a cemetery of dead religions. . . . It is the systematization and adaptation of ancient beliefs in accord with the new social principle" which came in with the fall of the Roman Empire. The only reason why the older religions gave way before Christianity was that they ceased to be in harmony with the economic conditions and social order of a later date.

"The Roman Catholic Church, which suited feudal times, in turn became undermined by a set of new economic forces with Protestantism as the result."

"In the light of historical facts," says this pamphlet, "Socialism v. Religion," "it is clear that religion has evolved continuously under the pressure of natural causes, and in this it does not differ from all other things; but a distinct characteristic is exhibited by religion's modern phase. In contrast with science, which grows in volume, complexity, interdependence, and definiteness, religion decreases in volume, cohesion, and definiteness, and is now in process of evolution — if such it can truly be called — into nothingness. It is, in fact, more accurately an evaporation than an evolution. . . ."

"It gives point, moreover, to the truth uttered by Naquet that: whenever knowledge takes a step forward God takes a step backward."

"It is therefore a profound truth," continues this socialist classic, "that Socialism is the natural enemy of religion;" and it is the writer's proud boast that "the entry of Socialism is, consequently, the exodus of religion. . . . Socialism as a system of society means the end of supernatural beliefs."

Socialism, we must not forget, is based on pure monism, whereas, "all religious teaching," as the pamphlet before us points out, "is directly opposed to the scientific materialism, or monism, which is an integral part of socialist philosophy."

We are again and again reminded that, "the materialist concept is the socialist key to history," and being directly antagonistic to all religious philosophy, it is destined, so we are assured, "to drive this philosophy and all its superstitions from their last ditch."

We are furthermore told in this declaration of the principles of the Socialist Party in Great Britain that: "If a man supports the Church, or in any respect allows religious ideas to stand in the way of the principles of Socialism or the activity of the Party, he proves thereby that he does not accept Socialism as fundamentally true and of the first importance, and his place is outside. No man can be consistently both a socialist and a Christian. It must be either the socialist or the religious principle that is supreme, for the attempt to couple them equally betrays charlatanism or lack of thought. There is, therefore, no need for a specifically anti-religious test. So surely does the acceptance of Socialism lead to the exclusion of the supernatural, that the Socialist has little need for such terms as Atheist, Free-thinker, or even Materialist; for the word Socialist, rightly understood, implies one who on all such questions takes his stand on positive science, explaining all things by purely natural causation; Socialism being not merely a politico-economic creed, but also an integral part of a consistent world philosophy."

With very good reason does the compiler of this party pamphlet close his work by once more assuring his readers that: "Our question is therefore answered. Socialism, both as a philosophy and as a form of society, is the antithesis of religion."

I have quoted at length from this manifesto about Socialism and Religion, recently put forth by the S. P. G. B., because I want you now listening to me to recognize what is the real, uncompromising attitude of the dyed-in-the-wool Socialist towards religion — more especially towards all revealed religion.

After indorsing the utterances I have put before you, well may thoroughgoing Socialists throw ridicule upon all such sayings as, "Socialism has no more to do with a man's religion than it has with the colour of his hair" (J. Ramsay Mac-Donald, "Socialism," p. 101), and "I first learned my Socialism in the New Testament, where I still find my chief inspiration" (Keir Hardie, 1900, Merthyr boroughs).

In spite of Keir Hardie's profession of faith, modern Socialists proclaim throughout their multitudinous press and in their heated harangues that they believe in no Redeemer, but that they believe in Redemption; that no man, no Saviour, no God in human form, can redeem the humanity of the day; that there is only one way of redeeming humanity — that humanity itself by labouring for humanity is to save humanity.

Again, are we not told that it is Socialism which preaches the gospel of redemption, but not of redemption through the Messiah, but through the work of socialistic principles? Once more, we are assured that the true Saviour has not come yet, but when he does come he will come in the shape of the world-redeeming principle of Socialism. I do not hesitate to say that always and everywhere, at home and abroad, you will find the popular socialist leader crying out before a group of his fellow-believers : "Away with this cant of clergy, this gospel about starlands, this wait-till-the-next-world kind of religion. We want no Christ, with His miracles of loaves and fishes in a day gone by ; what we want and what we intend to have is our share of this world's goods, here and now. We ask for no draft upon the bank of Heaven. Our Heaven is here and we will have it, we will no longer be fooled out of it by the capitalist." Not only will Socialism have nothing to do with re-vealed religion, but with Schäffle I am disposed to believe that even social Democracy would per-mit no freedom to religion and religious life. A socialist State would, of necessity, be far more intolerant than any existing State. The Paris Commune has not faded from our memory.

Liebknecht, who discovered that direct attack on religion was a bad political move, declared at the Halle Congress that : "Instead of squandering our strength in a struggle with the Church and Sacerdotalism, let us go to the root of the matter. We desire to overthrow the State of the classes. When we have done that the Church and Sacerdotalism will fall with it, and in this respect we are much more radical and much more definite in purpose than our opponents, for we like neither the priests nor the anti-priests." "Religion," writes Bebel ("Woman"), "will disappear by itself, without any violent attack."

But I cannot close the list without adding the testimony of a well-known American socialist writer, possibly the best equipped man in America to speak for his comrades and help them out of a difficulty. John Spargo in his book, "The Spiritual Significance of Modern Socialism," p. 88, tells us that the association of Socialism with atheism was an accidental result of the confluence of two streams of nineteenth-century thought. He excuses the founders of Socialism for attacking a Christianity which they thought was static, fixed, and resting on immutable dogmas. But he then informs us that all this has changed, that we have now discovered that Religion is a thing that is ever changing, and that the form of Christianity is undergoing its mutation through "the centuries of growth and intellectual progress." With him Christianity is a stage only in the process of soul evolution.

Christianity is to-day just what it was when rejected by the founders of Socialism. Modern dis·

N

covery has left its dogmas just where they were two centuries ago. The founders of Socialism knew what real Christianity meant, and they made no mistake in singling it out as their most dreaded enemy. John Spargo may be right in telling us that Socialism will fit in with the *new* Christianity, with the Christianity of the evolutionist and the modernist, with the Christianity that will exist when dogma is done away with, and which may be found outside the Catholic Church, possibly a hundred years from now. What kind of Christianity this will be we do not now care to say. But of this we are sure, that Socialism does not fit in with the *old* Christianity, with the Christianity which, like Christ, is ever the same; with the Christianity for which the martyrs shed their blood, and for which millions of Christians would gladly and proudly shed their blood to-day. How many, I ask, would shed their blood for the new Christianity which is put forward as the slave of time and change, and lays aside its dogmas just as a man does his winter garments, and which, under the guidance of men like John Spargo, puts in the same category of great men Karl Marx, Martin Luther, and Jesus Christ? With this shifting kind of Christianity we are not concerned at present. But we are concerned with the socialist movement.

We say the Catholic Church measures this movement in its essential features, observing its basic suppositions, investigating its inner spirit, analyzing its plausible but fallacious explanations. The Church of Christ has her hand upon its pulse, she has taken its temperature, she has diagnosed its condition, and she declares without passion, but without hesitation, that the actual living thing called Socialism is prejudicial to man's spiritual welfare, and that the danger has not ceased to exist even though the blunt anti-Christian utterances of the more outspoken Socialists have, in some quarters, been modified to an assurance that to Socialism "religion is nothing more than a private concern." What is this assurance worth when weighed in the balance of facts? It is not worth the paper on which it is stated.

I do not deny that there may be a few Catholics, especially in Europe, who are in an honest state of doubt as to whether the Church's denunciation of Socialism extends to certain milder forms of that doctrine which are sometimes to be found, and which claim to be merely economic and constitutional methods of curing evils which all of us admit to be intolerable. But a wider view of the matter will, we doubt not, enlighten them as to the real questions at issue. They will come, let us sincerely hope, to see the danger of taking even an indirect part in a movement which is characteristically opposed to the highest interests of mankind. It is impossible for the average Catholic man to stand his ground; he gets swept off his feet and becomes carried away by the movement. With those persons who write assuring me that Socialism has not interfered with their religion, I am not for the moment concerned.

I shall be told that in England, at all events, Socialism has, as a rule, no anti-Christian implications. It assumes no materialistic philosophy, and stands aloof altogether from questions of religion.

I answer first that in point of fact this is not so. The Socialism which the people know, the Socialism which is being assiduously pumped upon our toiling classes from platform and street corners and press, takes, in the main, the same view of human destiny and of religious truth as does the Socialism of the S. P. G. B. It is an international movement of common origin and progress. Its ethical outlook is always and everywhere the same.

This is a statement which we have already in part verified. We are not dealing with abstractions and considering what *might* be. We are witnessing an agitation which is being carried on in our midst by men and women organized in certain definite societies with ascertainable aims and programmes, methods and ideals. Let us therefore look at the chief bodies which make up the socialist army, say, in England, and see whether or not their aims and ideals are any more compatible than those of Socialists abroad with the teaching of Christianity.

Let us begin with the Social Democratic Federation which, I may assure you, is pouring its literature over our wage-earning classes and representing itself (not without some reason) as the real Socialism, the genuine article, true red Marxian, and allied with the great movement on the continent.

Mr. Wells admits that the Socialism of the S. D. F. is to this day "strongly anti-Christian in tone." We need scarcely allege evidence to prove so notorious a fact. A glance at the literature published by the revolutionary body should be enough to put the matter beyond all dispute.

Let us pass to the second and more important socialist body, the Independent Labour Party. It is more important because it is, as a matter of fact, succeeding to some extent in organizing the working classes, which the S. D. F. appears unable to do on any appreciable scale. The Independent Labour Party is generally admitted to be working on lines which, as Mr. Hunter points out, brings it into line with the most advanced Socialism of the continent, without alarming those to whom the outspoken principles of continental Socialism would be distasteful.

As a matter of fact, the work of organization which is going forward with such rapidity under the auspices of the I. L. P. often disguises from the eyes of the plain man the real aim for which the I. L. P. is steadily working. Hence, in order to discover the true inwardness of this movement we must go, not to the plain, blunt, and unsuspicious member, but to the leaders themselves; and from them we shall find the issues plainly enough stated.

To what spirit, then, are the members of the I. L. P. being moulded? What is their attitude towards Christianity?

"The Independent Labour Party is a socialist organization," writes Mr. Keir Hardie, its founder, "and for most of us Socialists is a religion. . . . To 99 per cent of the members of the I. L. P Socialism comes with all the emotional power of a great religious truth. . . . Man is at bottom a religious enthusiast lured on by his vision of a Kingdom of God upon earth. Nothing else explains the enthusiasm of the I. L. P." ("The I. L. P. All About It," p. 3.)

But what is the nature of this "religion" which

the I. L. P. is bent on fostering? We fear that not all even of its members realize what it involves. In the first place, the I. L. P. is, as Mr. Hardie points out in the same pamphlet, an international party (p. 12), in touch with the representatives of Socialism abroad, of that "continental Socialism" which, as Mr. Wells has told us, is "strongly anti-Christian in tone." What is more, it devotes a considerable amount of its energies to the task of initiating the British workmen into the specifically anti-Christian conceptions of continental Socialism. A glance at its authorized publications will make this clear, a perusal of its "classics" will satisfy you.

We may point out, too, that the I. L. P. is responsible for circulating Blatchford's attacks on Christianity (cf. *Labour Leader* for October 4, 1907, and Mr. Glasier's admissions) and the atheistic publications of the rationalist press. What does all this mean? It is not without significance.

I am well aware that the I. L. P., at their council meeting held on October the 4th and 5th of 1907, adopted the following resolution : —

"The National Council of the Independent Labour Party repudiates the attack upon Socialism on the ground that Socialism is opposed to religion, and declares that the socialist movement embraces men and women of all religions and forms of belief, and offers the most complete freedom in this respect within its ranks."

We fear that this means very little. It means no more than did the declarations of the Erfurt Programme that "religion is declared to be a private concern," or the previous declaration of the Gotha Programme that "religion is ruled to be a private matter." Similar resolutions are not unfrequently passed in socialist gatherings with a view to disarming suspicion. How are they to be interpreted? By the socialist ideals and by the socialist practice. What practical indication have Socialists ever given that they would be prepared to respect the religious convictions of others in the event of a socialist régime? What becomes of the workingman's religion after he has enlisted in the ranks of Socialism?

The German Socialists have, in their programmes, made religion a private affair. But the German Socialists lose no opportunity of attacking the Christian religion and doing their best to uproot it. Hence, when English Socialists declare that they too would have religion to be a private affair, we look not to words but to their practical interpretation. And we find the practical interpretation to be the same in both countries.

The visible Catholic Church is disliked and maligned equally in Italy and France, and in England and America no less. In my travels through the States I have made a practice of buying socialist papers in circulation. In most copies of them I found vile attacks upon religion; if not always direct, at least indirect, attacks.

I have referred to the S. D. F. and the I. L. P. Now what of Mr. Blatchford and his *Clarion?* It may be urged that Mr. Blatchford and the *Clarion* are not English Socialism. I reply that they stand for the Socialism with which thousands of British workingmen are being indoctrinated. You may not be familiar with the nature and extent of Mr. Blatchford's propaganda. Let me tell you that over a million copies of "Merrie England" have been sold. A very large number of workingmen allow Mr. Blatchford to do their thinking for them. These men will control the nation, so far as is in their power, on Mr. Blatchford's lines. The *Clarion* and its allied publications must certainly be taken into account when forming an estimate of the actual relations of Socialism to Christianity in England: for it is the Socialism of a very large number of men, and it would find its expression in actual measures were the cause of Socialism to triumph.

Mr. Wells is much distressed at the unsympathetic attitude of the Catholic Church towards Socialism. He gently insinuates that it may be due to a misapprehension.

"It is said, indeed, that a good Catholic of the Roman Communion cannot also be any sort of a Socialist. Even this very general persuasion may not be quite correct. I believe the papal prohibition was originally aimed entirely at a specific form of Socialism, the Socialism of Marx, Engels, and Bebel, which is, I must admit, unfortunately strongly anti-Christian in tone, as is the Socialism of the British Social Democratic Federation to this day. It is true that many leaders of the Socialist Party have also been Secularists, and that they have mingled their theological prejudices with their political work. This is the case not only in Germany and America, but in Great Britain, where Mr. Robert Blatchford, of the *Clarion*, for example, has carried on a campaign against doctrinal Christianity. But this association of Secularism and Socialism is only the inevitable throwing together of two sets of ideas because they have this in common, that they run counter to generally received opinions: there is no other connection (pp. 197, 198). . . . Perhaps, after all, the Church does not mean by

Socialismus Socialism as it is understood in English: perhaps it simply means the dogmatical, anti-Christian Socialism of the Continental type" (p. 139).

But since Socialism is an international movement with close international relations, the fact that the "Continental type" of Socialism is dogmatically anti-Christian is not without interest for ourselves, especially in view of the eagerness with which English and American Socialists copy continental patterns. And what, after all, is "Socialism as it is understood in English?" Mr. Wells has given away at one fell swoop the S. D. F., "many leaders of the Socialist party" even in Great Britain, and Mr. Blatchford of the *Clarion*. He might, as we have seen, have added the I. L. P.

Now what does Socialism mean to the British workingman, if it does not mean the *Clarion*, the S. D. F., the I. L. P., and the S. P. G. B.?

Mr. Wells, in order to reassure us, points triumphantly to the Fabian Society, and in particular to Fabian tracts by Dr. Clifford and the Rev. Stewart Headlam and also to Rev. R. J. Campbell's "Christianity and Social Order." With these and other "Christian Socialists" I shall deal in another Conference. But I may say at once that no serious student of the movement will regard them as possessing any influence in the evolution of the Socialism that counts. Socialism "as it is understood in English " is not the Socialism of Mr. Headlam and his friends, nor is it ever likely to be.

We are told, then, by Mr. Wells that there is no reason for alarm. True, continental Socialism is secularistic, the S. D. F. is secularistic, the I. L. P. and the S. P. G. B. are secularistic (see their programmes), the *Clarion* is secularistic, "many Socialist leaders in Great Britain are secularistic," but the Fabian Society has no such theological prejudice. The Fabian Society has made the required distinction between "two entirely separate thought-processes," and to the Fabian Society we may safely commit ourselves.

Now although the Fabian Society has exercised a very considerable influence among a certain class of people in the matter of socialist education and propaganda, it has not so much as attempted to organize politically the working classes. Mr. Robert Hunter (a shrewd and well-informed American socialist writer) points out that the Fabians have, from the socialist point of view, advanced no further than the position of the French Socialists before 1848; and he does not conceal his conviction that they are "Utopians" who are outside the real currents of socialist thought.

"To have a history of agitation in London (he says) extending over twenty-seven years, and to show at the end of that period no definite political organization of the working classes, is perhaps the most damaging evidence against the Fabian policy." ("Socialists at Work," p. 205.)

Mr. Hunter consoles himself with the reflection that there are few Socialists outside England who advocate Fabian tactics (p. 108).

Hence, even were it true that the Fabians keep their Socialism free from secularism, we should not feel perfectly reassured. For the Fabians, suggestive and interesting as they may be, do not control the swelling tide of English Socialism.

However, Mr. Wells has appealed to the Fabians and to the Fabians we shall go. Of the clergymen who have written Fabian tracts I shall speak presently; it will be seen that they increase rather than diminish our conviction as to the secularist implications of Socialism. But what of the other Fabians? Do they keep their secularism out of their Socialism?

Let us take Fabian Tract No. 72, *The Moral Aspect of Socialism*, by Mr. Sidney Ball, M.A., of St. John's College, Oxford.

"It would be idle to deny (he writes) that Socialism involves a change which would be almost a revolution in the moral and religious attitude of the majority of mankind. We may agree with Mill that it is impossible to define with any sort of precision the coming modification of moral and religious ideas. We may further, however, agree that it will rest (as Comte said) upon the solidarity of mankind (as represented by the Idea of State) " (p. 23).

Socialism, then, *involves* a change in religion and it is to base its religion upon the Idea of the State. Hence Socialism, as interpreted by a distinguished Fabian, *has* theological implications, and its religion (or substitute for religion) is not that of Christ but of Comte.

Of Mr. Bernard Shaw, the most widely known of the Fabian writers, little need be said. I would only observe that his flippant irreverence and anti-Christian bias are not merely exhibitions of personal bad taste. They are regarded by himself as part of his socialistic message.

I shall take one more example from the ranks of the Fabians, and this time it will be Mr. Wells himself. Despite his invitation to Catholic flies that they should walk into his socialistic parlour, the contents of that parlour are not such as to reassure those of us who retain a belief in revealed religion. True, he is convinced that

"Christianity involves . . . a practical Socialism if it is honestly carried out." ("New Worlds for Old," p. 197.) But the Christian ideal is, he goes on to tell us, the ideal of William Morris's, "News from Nowhere" (*ibid.*, p. 255), which again is the ideal of every man with "a full sense of beauty." But Christianity watered down to æsthetics is not the Christianity with which we are in any way concerned.

Mr. Wells is careful to tell us what might be expected to happen to the Catholic Church under a socialist régime. We will select but one point of his forecast.

"There seems no objection and no obstacle in Socialism," he says, "to religious houses, to nunneries, to monasteries, and the like, so far as these institutions are compatible with personal freedom and the public health, but of course factory laws and building laws will run through all these places, and the common laws and limitations of contract overrides their vows if their devotees repent. So you see Socialism will touch nothing living of religion." (*Ibid.*, p. 330.)

This is charmingly ingenuous! The State is to determine how much of religion is living and how much is dead. I fear that the average Socialist starts with a certain prejudice in the matter. Even so temperate a writer as Mr. Wells apparently fails to realize that some matters are subject to laws which transcend the common contract law "whenever the contracting parties repent."

Mr. Wells's socialist parlour would seem to contain a Procrustean bed for the benefit of Catholics. Yet even that is better than what they would find awaiting them in the parlour of the complete Socialist, — to wit, a guillotine.

This brings us to the whole question as to how Christianity might be expected to fare under Socialism. I will confine myself to the case of Catholics (for with their case I am chiefly concerned), though much of what I shall have to say may give matter for reflection to all who retain any belief in revealed religion.

Let us suppose that the socialist régime has been established, either violently (as the S. D. F. advocate) or by a peaceful process of Fabian permeation. The House of Commons, we will imagine, has an overwhelming socialist majority, the Crown and the Lords are abolished, and Socialists rule the London county council and all municipal bodies.

And now what is to be done about the Catholic religion? The question will have to be settled by

men who resemble the members of existing socialist bodies, — by men, that is to say, whose attitude towards Catholicism varies from an intense
and even virulent opposition to a frank disdain,
or, at best, to a complete inability to understand
the position of those to whom the supernatural is
the most real thing of which man has knowledge.

A little acquaintance with history will reveal
the fact that when religious legislation is framed
by men who are not alive to the inwardness of
religion, the "left wing" generally has its own way.
For the "left wing" is consistent and has a simple
and definite programme, — *Ecrasez l'infâme*, or
something equally drastic, — while the rest of the
governing body can but propose a compromise
which is apt to be half-hearted. So the consistent
section generally gets its way. Its point might be
illustrated by the history of more than one Liberal
Government on the continent of recent years.
Had Catholics of England during the past few
years been a little less determined, we might have
been able to illustrate the point by an example
nearer home.

However, let us suppose that this is not the
case. Let us imagine that, contrary to all the
tendencies which the main currents of Socialism
have always and everywhere displayed, the work

o

of discovering a *modus vivendi* for belated super-naturalists is confided to a committee consisting of a number of men as well-intentioned and un-prejudiced as Mr. H. G. Wells. I will not even embarrass their task by adding a sprinkling of Drs. Cliffords and Revv. Campbells.

Now, what will be the task in front of these gentlemen, and how can they accomplish it so as to allow to Catholics an even tolerable existence?

"The heavy social burdens that oppress re-ligious bodies (says Mr. Wells) will (in a socialist State) be altogether lifted from them. They will have no poor to support, no schools, no hospitals, no nursing sisters; the advance of civilization will have taken over these duties which Christianity first taught us to realize."

But here difficulties begin to thicken about the heads of our well-intentioned committee. After all, they cannot put a million Lancashire folk and four hundred thousand Londoners into the lethal chamber. And until they do so they will find these among the number of British subjects (a number which shows no sign of diminishing, in spite of rationalist propaganda) in set rebellion against certain items of Mr. Wells's good-natured pro-gramme: "The religious bodies will have . . . to support . . . no schools." There will indeed be little opposition on the part of the religious bodies to the proposal that they should not *support* their schools. Were this alone intended, Mr. Wells would indeed be a benefactor. But we fear that the emphasis is on the "have," — Catholics would *have* no schools either to support or to control. This state of things they would emphatically resist.

I cannot here go into the whole weary question of education. Suffice to say, that although the Catholic demand for Catholic teaching, in Catholic schools, by Catholic teachers, is demonstrably just and is in fact the only solution which can bring peace to any educationally distracted country, yet it is almost impossible to drive into the heads of those who have not a glimmering as to what Catholicism is all about, the notion that the Catholic demand for Catholic education is a reasonable demand. The secularist — even the well-meaning secularist — commonly persists in thinking that we harbour a prejudice in favour of obscurantism and inferior sewage. Let us hear Mr. Wells himself ; he is considering the effects which would follow "a reaction" in favour of parental rights : —

"Subject to the influence of a powerful and well-organized Church, a rejuvenescent Church, he, the father, is to resume that control over wife and children of which the modern State has partially deprived him. The development of a secular education is to be arrested, particular stress is to be laid upon the wickedness of any intervention with natural reproductive processes, the spread of knowledge in certain directions is to be made criminal, and early marriages are to be encouraged. . . . I do not by any means regard this as an impossible programme; I believe that in many directions it is quite a practicable one; it is in harmony with great masses of feeling in the country, and with many natural instincts. It would not, of course, affect the educated wealthy and leisurely upper class in the community, who would be able and intelligent enough to impose their own private glosses upon its teaching, but it would 'moralize' the general population, and reduce them to a state of prolific squalor. Its realization would be, I believe, almost inevitably accompanied by a decline in sanitation, and a correlated rise in birth-rate and death-rate, for life would be cheap and drain-pipes and antiseptics dear." ("Socialism and the Family," pp. 53-55.)

But is there really any necessary connection between the vindication of due parental rights and bad drainage: or do we religiously cultivate squalor, and all disease-producing microbes? Catholics want, like others, to reduce squalor. But there is something about which they are still more anxious: they pay their ungrudging tribute of admiration and gratitude for the municipal trolley and for cheap fares to children—but they want Catholic education for their children much more than cheap transportation. "I won't have my children growing up into irreligious products of a godless school," is possibly the form in which their prejudice might be expressed. And some acquaintance with secularist education might explain their warmth of feeling in the matter. We know something of the profanity and lack of reverence, the bad manners and worse talk, that is fostered in many an elementary school where drainage is perfect, the microbe rare, and appurtenances are magnificent: and we contrast them with the joyous innocence, the honesty and the respect for self and others which for the most part are to be found in schools taught by Religious who have to struggle with poverty. Consult unprejudiced school inspectors on either side of the Atlantic, and you will understand what I say.

Truth to tell, Socialism and Christianity cannot come together; they move in opposite directions; they are as much apart as Earth and Heaven.

VI

SOCIALISM AND CHRISTIAN SOCIALISTS

IT is altogether unnecessary to draw out a long thesis to show that Christian Socialism is a form of Collectivism repudiated by all thorough-going Socialists. It is a contradiction in terms. It says one thing and means another. The man-in-the-street assures me that the Christian Socialist is tolerated only by the vote catcher. "We have got no use for him," said a goldminer to me at Dawson. "Why not?" asked I. "Well," he continued, " it is like this. If he is a real nugget, a church-going Christian, he is looking beyond what we are. He's a Northern Light, he is. What we want, is no sky-piloted Socialist, but on the contrary, we believe in the man who is whole-hearted on the job. We have a class-basis for our Socialism. We have class-hatred, no lying brotherhood, promising two heavens, one down here, and the other up there." "Till Socialism gets hold of the heart," said another, " it is not going to be busy for the workingman; it is not his religion, and till

it is we have no use for him." Everywhere, from
the Hudson to the Yukon, I found the wage-earning Socialist to be the same dead-earnest apostle,
believing in his mission, and prepared to make un-
limited sacrifices to promote its interests and to
extend its boundaries. One man told me that
Socialism was like mining, it obsessed you, it dissatisfied you for anything else, it buoyed you up
and made you feel, as nothing else did, that life
was worth living, and that one day you would strike
gold and put the present robber millionnaire in his
right place. "It may not come in my time,"
concluded my friend in overalls, "but it is rising,
as sure as the tide, and before my children are
through, the thing will be straightened out and
there will be but one class in the States — the
working class, with plenty to go round, and to
spare."

I suggested that it was the money and not the
work that the Socialist wanted to go round, and
that if men refused to work, there certainly would
not be enough to go round. I told him that on
the ship which had brought me to the Northland
the quartermaster had said to me that it was not
at all likely he and his mates were going to work as
a crew, if, after their time was served, they were
to be called upon to divide up their pay with

loafers and loiterers on shore. "What we are all looking for is a bit of a home of our own, with bits of green stuff to brighten our store windows, and a tidy bit to put by for our own when we are gone. Be sure of this," he went on to say, "we sea-faring men have got grit and sand in us, and we don't want anybody else's dimes; we want our own, and it's up to us to shake off this Socialism which is only bred in idle bones, and in the men on the wharf who make a sorry face when you land, and want the loan of a dollar which they never offer to pay. When there's anything doing, they close up like clams."

My Northland miner was not to be put off. He believed that the loiterer and tramp were bred of discontent, that when their circumstances and opportunities would improve, they too would improve. He quoted Lloyd George and his denunciations of the "idle rich," and declared that the working class had as much claim to idle as rich men, but that when the reign of Socialism should dawn, there would be no more idlers, no more unemployed or unemployables.

It is quite surprising to find among Socialists an almost universal belief in the innate goodness and industry of man, and in the assumption that it is the present iniquitous state of society which has dissatisfied, degraded, and depraved the faulty brother.

I spoke with another Alaskan Socialist at Ketchekan — I was looking over the creek bridge where 10,000 salmon, so thick that you could not see the bottom of the stream, were fighting their way up the rapids to lay their spawn in the sand banks beyond. There they were battling for dear life, it taking some of them four days to win as many yards.

I turned to my socialist friend and observed: "Here is an equal opportunity for all, but I notice it is only the strong and the strenuous salmon that force their way and forge to the front. Is not this wondrous sight a picture of what happens in the human race?" He turned to me and said: "Socialism is going to make it easy for all. When we have socialized all the instruments of the production of wealth, there will be a living for all; then hustling will be at an end; none will have to lay back." He told me Socialism was growing all the time, and that there were thousands of Catholics among them in Alaska. I asked him whether he believed in Christian Socialism. He smiled, and said they claimed to have them in Chicago, where they published a paper called *The Christian Socialist*, but they were of no more use than a prairie dog. Socialism was all or nothing. It was the best religion that ever was started, and it was going to win. One thing is sure, and it is this, that the workingman on this continent believes there must be a change, and he will tell you that no matter what you have against Socialism you will have to give it a chance. "It may not be the best solution of the difficulty," said a group of Western cowboys, "but it's the best as we know of. It can't be worse than the present state of things, and if we give it a square deal, it will most likely be far better for all of us. Anyway, it's coming, and we are in with it."

Another little group of men from the copper mines informed me that they had been working for seven weeks, and had laid aside 200 dollars each which they would "fire," or spend in less than a week at Seattle. "We are like this ship," said one; "we load up to unload; when we are through with our 'poke' we will return for another freight." I expostulated with them and argued how much better it would be for them and for their characters, if, like the beaver, the squirrel, the woodpecker, the ant, and the bee, they banked what they could spare, becoming like them thriving, provident capitalists. They replied that thrift was no plank in the socialist programme; that it was better to be "down and out" than to hoard like a miser. When Socialism came in, there would be one crime only, capital. Meanwhile they did as they willed with their own.

These happy-go-lucky bread earners, who live from hand to mouth, who will spend hundreds a night in a saloon, and when broken and turned out, quietly return to work till they have loaded up for another spill, are mere tools in the hand of the soap-box socialist orator. They greedily gulp down all he says, and readily believe in the forthcoming millenium which he promises. They have little outlook beyond the realms of hippodromes, saloons, and dime-theatres.

Mr. Charles E. Russell, socialist candidate for governor of New York last year, was not hitting beyond the mark when he said: "To these men and women, Socialism does not mean a political party organized to win elections and to secure offices: *Socialism is to them a religion.*" For the most part they know none other.

Joseph Leatham in his work, "Socialism and Character," does not hesitate to say, "I cannot remember a single instance of a person who is at once a really earnest Socialist and an orthodox Christian."

The *New York Call*, March 2, 1911, reminds

its readers that: "There is nothing to be gained by holding out false hopes that a study of Socialism does not tend to undermine religious beliefs. The theory of economic determinism alone," it goes on to say, "if thoroughly grasped, leaves no room for a belief in the supernatural." We are reminded, too, in a tract called *Christian Socialism* (p. 23) that "no Christian who accepts the Ten Commandments as the basis of the moral law can possibly deny the right of private individual property. If the Christian Socialist admits this, he is no Socialist; if he denies it, he is no Christian." "The contradiction in terms," writes the author of "Socialism and Religion," "known as the Christian Socialist is inevitably antagonistic to working-class interests and the waging of the class struggle. His avowed object is usually to purge the socialist movement of its materialism, and this, as we have seen, means to purge it of its Socialism and to divert it from its material aims to the fruitless chasing of spiritual will-o'-the-wisps." He concludes with the remark that: "A Christian Socialist is, in fact, an anti-Socialist."

In this pamphlet published by "the Socialist Party of Great Britain" and already referred to is found the following paragraph :—

"The inflexible laws of the known universe cannot logically be held to cease where our immediate experience ends, to make way for an unscientific concept of an uncaused and creating Being. The Creation idea is unsupported by evidence, and is in conflict with every scientific law. Socialism is consistent only with that monistic view which regards all phenomena as expressions of the underlying matter-force reality and as parts of the unity of Nature which interact according to inviolable laws. It is the application of science, the archenemy of religion, to human social relationships; and just as the basic principle of the philosophy of Socialism finds itself in conflict with religion, so does it, as a propagandist movement, find religion acting against it."

The pamphlet continues: —

"The main reason for capitalists' liberality toward religious bodies is plain. They know that religion is incompatible with Socialism, and look upon it rightly as a working-class soporific; indeed, as Marx said, 'religion is the opium of the people.' And it is thus the agent of class domination, not only because of its beliefs and organization, but also, in spite of opinions to the contrary, by virtue of the ethics with which it is associated. The teaching of the Gospels, so far from supporting Socialism, is directly hostile to it."

The dyed-in-the-wool Socialist is aggressive in his denunciation of the ethics of the Christian Socialist. He says: "The asceticism, self-abnegation, and professed other-worldliness of Christian teaching, which regards this earth as a vale of tears and a painful preparation for a life in the clouds, is an ethic of slavish degradation; and when taught to the workers, it admirably reflects the narrowest self-interest of the exploiting class. It is an ethic that runs counter to working-class interests at every point. It is the counterpart, not indeed of a communist, but of an individualist society." As an eminent prelate said at the 1909 Church Congress at Swansea, "Individualism is of the very essence of Christianity." And Christianity, we may add, is by the same token the very antithesis of Socialism.

I have shown that Socialism, the actual living Socialism which is preached in the highways and poured from the popular press, is a Socialism which is antagonistic to Christianity. Sometimes the antagonism is displayed openly and defiantly, as in the case of the Social Democratic Party. Sometimes it is encouraged in practice and deprecated in theory, as in the case of the Independent Labor Party. Sometimes, again, it is wrapped up in semi-scientific language, and we are told with calm assurance that in future the "Idea of the State" will probably give us all the religion we shall want.

But I shall be told that Christian Socialists have for their aim and object the conversion of Socialists from their gross materialism. Here it will be said is a movement which will christianize English and American Socialism and deflect it from its continental atheism. I shall be reminded that clergymen have written Fabian Tracts, that Pan-Anglican Congresses are largely tinged with Socialism, that a hundred and fifteen Christian ministers have signed a socialist manifesto, that a number of advocates of Socialism have been found at Free Church Councils, that the Christian Social Union harbours many socialist members, that the Christian Socialist League comprises none but socialist members, — that, in short, the Christian Socialist is abroad.[1]

---

[1] The Rev. S. Proudfoot in the *Church Socialist Quarterly* (of which he is editor) for January, 1909, thus writes of one of the meetings at the Church Congress of 1908 : —

"It is hardly an exaggeration to say that if a vote on Socialism had been taken at the end of this meeting, a majority would have been found supporting it. After this no one can charge Socialism as being anti-Christian. Christians at this meeting were shown that Socialists were inspired by Christ" (p. 57).

I have not overlooked this movement. But as the result of a careful study of Christian Socialism in its various manifestations, I have come to two conclusions. The first is that the movement stands not the slightest chance of counteracting the predominantly anti-Christian tone of current Socialism. The second is that in so far as it is really socialistic and not merely social, it has cut the ground from under its feet by abandoning what is most characteristic and vital in Christianity.

Let me begin by paying my sincere tribute of praise to the generous spirit in which many clergymen of the Established Church, and of the Free Churches are endeavouring to grapple with social evils. Their sympathy with the poor and suffering must command the respect of all right thinking men. Too long have many Christians neglected the just grievances of the toiling and suffering classes, and all must welcome a movement in favour of Christian social reform. But in taking

"After this" we are not surprised to find the Reverend writer going on to tell how all "reactionary survivals were hushed when the Professor (Burkitt) ended his speech with what was really a scathing and prophetic denunciation of organized Christianity." That disorganized Christianity should ally itself with Socialism is, after all, not so very surprising.

to Socialism the clergymen in question are making an alliance with a power which they cannot control and which must eventually control them. And in doing this, are they not rejecting the mighty forces of social reform which Christianity has placed in their hands?

There is something pathetic in the way in which "Christian Socialists" are making efforts to ingratiate themselves with organized bodies of men who take no pains to conceal their hatred of Christianity. "Everywhere the aid of the Christian Socialist League was warmly welcomed by our brethren . . . of the S. D. P.," says a report of the Salford Branch of the Christian Socialist League. (*Church Socialist Quarterly*, January, 1909.)

"Our brethren of the S. D. P!" True, all men are our brethren, — or let us say our brothers, since we are reminded of the witty definition, *Brethren:* "an ecclesiastical noun of multitude, no connection with *brother.*" But this does not mean that we should be ready to assimilate all men's methods or share their eccentricities. Now the C. S. L. is only too anxious to coöperate with the S. D. P. as a society. We have already seen something of the S. D. P. and its assiduous railings at Christianity. How does it

P

reciprocate these touching marks of affection and confidence? Let us hear its leaders.

"Lastly, one word on that singular hybrid, the 'Christian Socialist.' . . . The association of Christianism with any form of Socialism is a mystery, rivalling the mysterious combination of ethical and other contradictions in the Christian divinity itself" (sic !). (Belfort Bax, "The Ethics of Socialism," p. 52.)

Christianity, according to Mr. H. M. Hyndman, the founder of the S. D. P., is practically a dead creed. Socialism is the only religion left. (Vide *Daily Express*, Feb. 1, 1908.)

These are scarcely the words of a man who welcomes the aid of Christians as such.

The workingman is being taught in popular pamphlets to reject any Christian flavour in his Socialism if he would have the real article. Sentences such as the following are not unfrequently to be met with in socialistic literature : —

"Let us make a stand against this persistent hankering after a Christian sanction for a system which carries its own sanction with it." ("Was Jesus a Socialist?" by James Leatham. Twentieth Century Press.)

This protest is no novelty; but Christian Socialists persist in shutting their ears to it, or ascribing to it a confusion of ideas in the socialist mind. We fear that the mental confusion lies elsewhere. They must recognize that the French are a logical people, so let me quote them some words of M. Millerand: —

"Socialism offers to our appetite for justice and goodness a purely human ideal completely disengaged from all dogma, and thus distinct, *without possibility of confusion* from Christian Socialism." ("Disc. de Saint-Mandé.")

Nor can it be said that the "Christian Socialists" have made any contribution to the cause of Socialism except in so far as they have increased the number of its adherents by blinding their spiritual charges to the real questions at issue. The socialist leaders want votes, and they will sometimes conceal their contempt of their clerical allies in order to use the latter as a cat's-paw by which to reach churchgoers. But with the exception of those cases in which their Christianity has completely evaporated under the action of their Socialism, the Christian Socialists have contributed little or nothing to the thought of the movement. It must be confessed that their economics and sociology commonly inspire as little confidence as their theology.

Let me repeat once more that I am speaking

of the "Christian Socialist," and not of those Christian social reformers who sometimes complicate an already confused problem by calling themselves Socialists, while expressly disavowing the fundamental tenets of Socialism. Long ago, at the Church Congress of 1890, the Bishop of Durham in his paper on "Socialism" said that he would "venture to employ it [the term Socialism] apart from its historical associations," and then proceeded to make it a mere synonym for coöperation. The Bishop might, of course, employ the term in any sense he liked; but what is the use of attempting to give a new meaning to a word which stands for a definite historical movement. Other Anglican bishops have, unfortunately, taken the same line. They have declared themselves Socialists, — but added that they do not believe in the transfer of all the means of production to the community. The result of this trifling has been that many socialist clergymen to-day are willing to throw themselves at the heads of any organized bodies labelled with the name of Socialist. They are ready, as the Rev. Stewart Headlam says, "to unite with Socialists of every sort," no matter, apparently, how definitely anti-Christian those Socialists may be in their methods and aims. Yet they " ought to be aware," as Mr. Roosevelt has written in the

Outlook, "of the pornographic propaganda of the movement."

"This attitude of ignorance and confusion on the part of the Church of England," writes Mr. Geoffrey Drage, M.P., "is in marked contrast to the expressed opposition of the Catholic Church." ("The Labour Problem," p. 380.)

But let me pass to my second and more serious criticism of the Christian Socialists. Not only are they incapable of deflecting English Socialism, but they have effaced from their own teaching those very characteristics which make Christianity a great social power. Not only is their Socialism feeble, but their Christianity is eviscerated.

For these Christian Socialists, whatever be their measure of good faith, are effectively betraying the cause of Christianity. They are putting forward as Christianity a view of Christ's mission and teaching which is directly contradictory to the Gospels, and is repudiated by the voice of Christian tradition. Of their appeal to the example of the early Church and to the Fathers I shall have something to say presently. Let me first examine their account of the Gospel message. It will not be difficult to show that they have robbed that message of its deepest truth, and deprived it of those very characteristics which have been the secret of its power.

Let me begin by sketching, in the simplest way, the purport of Christ's teaching as it is revealed in the New Testament and expounded by the voice of tradition. I shall not go beyond the substance of the penny catechism familiar to every child in a Catholic elementary school.

Jesus Christ, the Second Person of the Blessed Trinity, made man and born of the Virgin Mary, is our Redeemer. He came on earth "to redeem us from sin and hell and to show us the way to heaven." Man in consequence of the Fall had come under God's disfavour. He had forfeited the gifts given to Adam, including that chief gift by which he was raised from the condition of servant to that of a son of God. A divine satisfaction was required to redress the balance. Such satisfaction was found in the death of Christ. By it we are made once more sons of God and members of Christ's mystical body. If we have faith and are baptized, we are restored to that intimate communion, that ineffable friendship with God, of which the presence of the Holy Spirit in our souls is the pledge and the accomplishment.

Christ came to raise the human race to a supernatural life. He founded a Kingdom — the "Kingdom of God" — which transcends the material kingdom to which the more worldly minded of the Jews looked forward. His Kingdom was to be consummated in Heaven, but it was to have its beginnings on earth. It was to be a spiritual Kingdom, — a Kingdom of grace here and of glory hereafter; yet it was to have its visible expression here in His Church. Hence the term is sometimes applied to the consummated and glorious Kingdom in eternity, sometimes to the spiritual life within the soul which lifts men to this higher order, and sometimes again to the visible Church, the Kingdom on earth.

But in every case the Kingdom is a *supernatural kingdom*. It is a sphere of spiritual blessing and privilege. It demands repentance and faith. It is "otherworldly," for its consummation is in Heaven, — though the securing of that consummation involves the performance of duties here on earth.

What, then, is the aim of the whole Christian dispensation? What is the purport of Christ's teaching? It is to make of the individual a child of God, to sanctify his soul, to unite him to God, to give him an eternal destination and help him to reach it. As I have pointed out in another Conference, the Christian message is primarily for the individual and not for society. Christianity is democratic in this high sense that its chief stress is on the priceless value of the individual. And besides being a message to the individual, it is a spiritual message: it is concerned with the *soul* of the individual.

Hence its chief end is not man's well-being on earth. It regards temporal progress as quite insignificant except in so far as it is a means to everlasting life. It tells us that man has not here an abiding city, and that this life is a test and a trial for a life hereafter which is ineffably more important.

As a matter of fact, this Christian otherworldliness is by no means prejudicial to man's temporal prosperity. As I have shown in another Conference, the deeper our faith is in a life to come, the stronger will be our resolve to make justice reign in the world, to use our talents for the common good, to relieve misery and distress, and to make human existence a bright and beautiful thing. But the point to notice here is that Christianity from first to last, Christianity as preached by Christ and His apostles, by saints and by doctors in all ages, is concerned first and foremost with man's redemption and sanctification, with the raising of the individual to a sonship with God which shall be revealed only in the life to come.

The Christian Church starts with its belief in

the fall of man through Adam, and in his redemption through Christ. Socialism, on the contrary, opens its campaign with the philosophy of the innate goodness and rightness of man, teaching that it is not the regeneration of man's *heart* but of his *environment* that is most of all needed for his emancipation from all evil.

Now, then, let us turn to the "Christian Socialists" and see what is the caricature of Christianity upon which they endeavour to base their Socialism.

"What think ye of Christ? Whose Son is he?" was Our Lord's test question. Among the earliest heresies which the Church had to strangle were the heresies of those who denied that Christ was Divine, the Son of God, sent by the Father to do a work which only God could do.

What was Christ's work and mission on earth according to the "Christian Socialists"? Do they regard it as a supernatural work?

"It is extraordinary (says the Rev. Percy Dearmer, in Fabian Tract No. 133) how little many Christian people realize the meaning of their own religion so that they are actually shocked very often at Socialism; and yet all the while Socialism is doing just the very work which they have been commanded by their Master to do. This fact is so obvious that no representative and responsible Christian body can be found to deny it" (p. 3).

Mr. Dearmer apparently does not regard the Catholic Church as a "representative and responsible Christian body," for he must know that the Catholic Church has persistently denied that Socialism is doing the work which Christ commanded us to do.

The writer then proceeds to consider what he calls the "central features of Christianity," and endeavours to show that they all correspond with Socialism.

On page 5 he has the following note : —

"Let it be clearly understood. This Tract is not written to belittle the Godward side of religion, or to condone that lack of spirituality which is too common already. But its object is the duty to our neighbour, which is as much neglected as the duty to God."

But whatever may have been the author's intention in writing the Tract, the Tract itself does clearly belittle "the Godward side of religion." Not only is its whole stress on material well-being, but it distinctly conveys the impression that material well-being is the ultimate end of religious effort. Its theme is not duty to our neighbour in the Christian sense (an excellent text which much needs preaching) but duty to our neighbour in the socialistic sense. By an ingenious perversion of scriptural texts it reaches the conclusion that Christ's work on earth was identical with the work of socialist bodies.

Christ, we are told, was executed "because He preached revolutionary doctrines" (p. 4), — "the *Magnificat* was a revolutionary hymn" (p. 7). "St. John the Baptist told the people to practise communism." He did "just what Socialists are trying to do" (p. 5).

I may observe in passing that I have not yet met with any Fabian Tracts, or S. D. P. pamphlets, which, with St. John the Baptist, invite people to confess their sins and do penance. Nor is his advice to be content with one's pay, a main plank of the socialistic platform. St. John wanted to moralize, and spiritualize, existing institutions, not to sweep them away. His purpose was to change men's hearts rather than their incomes. He makes no attacks on private property, though he insists on its responsibilities, as the Catholic Church has always done and continues to do to-day.

The writer then goes on to consider the "four most prominent forms" of Christ's teaching, —

His Signs, His Parables, His Sermon, and His Prayer.

As to Christ's "Signs" we are told that "He devoted a large part of His time to fighting against disease and premature death" (p. 6). The expression "fighting against" is one which will scarcely commend itself to a believer in the Divinity of Christ. It suggests a limitation of Christ's omnipotence, and is quite inapplicable to the calm majesty of the Divine Wonder-worker. And to say that He "devoted a large part of his time" to this work suggests that His object was confined to a mere humanitarian alleviation of temporal misfortunes. No glimpse is offered us of the deep spiritual meaning of Christ's miracles of healing, — of His constant care to bring out their typical reference to that much more appalling evil, — sin.

"Death in youth," continues Mr. Dearmer, "is horrible, and so are sickness and deformity." True, these are things which we endeavour to prevent. They are, in themselves, physical evils. But to call them, in the concrete, necessarily "horrible" shows a strange insensibility to the real values of life. The death of the girl martyr St. Agnes is scarcely "horrible" to the Christian eye. We may add that the heroic death of a young soldier is not commonly called "horrible," even by those who are not Christians. Sad it may be; but it is also glorious. If St. Paul could glory in his infirmities, we too, amid all our efforts to relieve pain in a true spirit of Christian charity, may yet bless the mercy of God which will not remove all pain from our midst. Given our present nature, the world without pain would not be a very sympathetic place to live in. It is suffering that is always drawing us into closer union; it is the child's cry of pain which brings to its bedside the mother and the nurse. With no pang of pain to sound the alarm the doctor's aid might be all too late.

But the Rev. Mr. Dearmer's Fabian Tract only reëchoes the Rev. Mr. Headlam's Fabian Tract in which we read : —

"The death of a child, or a young man, or a man in the prime of life — that is a monstrous, a disorderly thing; not part of God's order for the world, but the result of wrong-doing somewhere or other. And if you want a rough description of the object of Christian Socialism, I should be bold to say that it was to get rid of premature death altogether " (p. 3).

If my readers want a rough description of the object of Christianity, I need no boldness to say that it is to get rid of everlasting death altogether, and to help all men, young and old, to meet physical death, when it comes to them, with Christian faith and confidence. The mother of the Maccabees would, it seems, have made a poor Christian Socialist!

But we must follow Mr. Dearmer a little further:—

"Our English Bible calls these acts miracles; but this is a mistranslation of the original Greek, which calls them *signs*—that is, significant acts."

The English Bible as a matter of fact also calls them signs,—and the original Greek has various terms for them which justify our calling them strictly *miracles*. But the point to notice here is that the writer gains nothing at all by calling them "signs." For a sign, as he himself points out, is a significant act. Now by reducing Christ's miracles to the level of humanitarian healings he robs them of all their significance. Christ wrought miracles—"signs"—to prove His divine mission, and not merely to remove physical suffering. This is their significance. Yet Mr. Dearmer continues:—

"All sanitary and social reform is but carrying out on a larger scale the signs which Our Lord wrought for our example" (p. 6).

This is amazing ! But it does not stand alone. Let us turn back to the Rev. Mr. Headlam's Fabian Tract. There we read, on pages 6 and 7, the following : —

" The Christian Church, therefore, is intended to be a society . . . *mainly and chiefly* [italics ours] for doing on a large scale throughout the world those secular socialistic works which Christ did on a small scale in Palestine."

Any Catholic child in an elementary school would reply, with the Christian saints and doctors of all ages, that the Church exists mainly and chiefly for nothing of the sort. The Catholic child would tell Mr. Headlam that it was the mission of Christ's Church first of all to teach the Divinity of the Teacher, and then, and as a consequence of it, the infallible character of His teaching. The child would know what Mr. Headlam does not, that the Christian Church is chiefly concerned with the spiritual welfare of its children though their material well-being concerns it no less.

Mr. Dearmer displays a similar perversity in his account of the Parables of Christ.

" And here I would point out the meaning of a whole series which are called the 'Parables of the Kingdom.' They expressly confute the common notion that the Kingdom of Heaven is something only in the next world, and that men are set only to save what Kingsley called 'their own dirty souls'" (p. 7).

True, the Kingdom of Heaven has its beginnings in this world, and we have to help to save the souls and bodies of our neighbours as well as our own. It is natural, too, that the earthly phase of the Kingdom should be most prominent in the Parables. But the Parables by no means confute the Christian notion that man's doings in this world derive their chief importance from their bearing on the next. As for Kingsley's phrase about men saving "their own dirty souls," it is, if we take it seriously, an offensive piece of ir-reverence against the solemn words of Christ Our Lord, — "What doth it profit a man if he gains the whole world and suffers the loss of his own soul?" Was it not for the priceless individual soul that our Saviour lived, bled, and died and rose again?

The phrase, "the Kingdom of God," is one which is frequently employed by Christian So-cialists as an equivalent of the socialist State. The new precursors of the Kingdom may be men who are filled with the bitterest hatred of Chris-tianity, — blasphemers to whom St. Paul would have given short shrift. That does not distress the Christian Socialist. Let us hear the Rev. R. J. Campbell : —

"I am rather keen on Robert Blatchford. I have an impression that he has done high service for England. He has preached the Kingdom of God." ("The New Theology and the Socialist Movement," p. 9.)

Mr. Blatchford (who does not believe in God) may well ask to be saved from his friends !

This socialistic use of the term, "Kingdom of God," is commonly a mere piece of empty rhetoric for which not a word of historical justification is offered. But sometimes, on the other hand, attempts are actually made to find in the Bible a justification for it.

Such writers start from the old Theocracy and argue from the detailed legislation thereof to the nature of the Kingdom which Christ came to found. Their fundamental mistake is the assumption that the Theocracy was a first stage of the Kingdom. Really it is sharply distinguished against it : "The Law and the Prophets were until John: from that time the Kingdom of God shall be preached." There is indeed a relation between them, but it is merely that of type and anti-type, the two being on completely different planes.

Q

I must be allowed to dwell in this matter for a space, since the mistake just alluded to is at the root of much wild talk among Christian Socialists about the realization of the Kingdom of God.

In the Theocracy God was the immediate and personal Ruler of the State, the Head of the civil government. Like any other wise legislator He laid down a number of positive laws to meet the special needs of that time and people. Included among these were the laws concerning land tenure on which some socialist writers lay much stress. But of the three classes of laws, judicial, ceremonial, and moral, for which there was divine sanction in the days of the Theocracy, only one, the moral, has a direct relation to the end of the Kingdom of Christ, — the "Ecclesia" of those who are by divine adoption the sons of God. The judicial and ceremonial laws of the Mosaic dispensation passed away with the old order. Indeed, purely economic legislation was bound to change with varying economic conditions of life. The law, for instance, of the Year of Jubilee, an example on which some stress has been laid, has no more a place in the unchangeable moral order instituted by God, than has the precept against eating the hare or the screech-owl, which also belongs to the positive law of the Theocracy.

Still more futile is the attempt to find a socialistic basis for the Kingdom in the denunciations of the Prophets. The prophet Isaias, a special favourite of the Christian Socialists, thunders against the oppression of the poor (any Catholic child could tell them that this is one of the "four sins crying to Heaven for vengeance"), but the oppression in question is the flagrant violation of the ordinary principles of justice as recognized alike by Socialist or individualist. I will quote some of the passages which are brought forward in support of socialistic tenets : —

"The princes are faithless, companions of thieves ; they all love bribes, they run after rewards. They judge not for the fatherless and the widow's cause cometh not into them" (i. 23).

"Wo to them that make wicked laws, and when they write, write injustice : to oppress the poor in judgment and do violence to the cause of the humble of my people : that widows might be their prey and that they might rob the fatherless" (x. 1, 2).

The rich and the ruling classes used a corrupt judicature to rob and oppress the poor. It needs the vivid imagination of a Socialist to see in the invectives of the Prophets against this horrible sin a divine warrant for Socialism.

Of a further type of Christian Socialism we need take little notice here, in that it has no claim to the title "Christian" as that word is ordinarily understood. We have an example of this in Rev. R. J. Campbell's book, "Christianity and the Social Order." The author denies to Our Lord any object whatsoever save that of material reform. The one essential message of Jesus, the message of the supernatural life, of the "one thing necessary," he not only ignores, but even denies its existence. Our Lord had no thought of a life beyond the tomb; He was concerned only with the future of men on earth. His answer to the Pharisees who asked, to which of the seven husbands she had successively the woman should belong "*in the resurrection,*" is thus commented on by Mr. Campbell : —

"He even seems to have thought that marriage and procreation would be at an end with the establishment of the Kingdom of God, although that establishment was to take place on earth."

Sin as between man and God is, to this writer, a figment of the theological imagination. The only sin that would seem to be recognized by Jesus is selfishness.

There is no serious attempt at proof. Mr. Campbell accepts as unquestionable the more extreme conclusions of the German rationalists, and simply ignores all the supernatural side of our Saviour's personality and teaching. How sad it is that he appears to be incapable of rising to anything higher than the world of sense.

To me it seems unnecessary to discuss a system built upon such premisses. Whatever may be said for it on economic grounds, it certainly does not merit the epithet "Christian," since its very foundation is the denial of all that is best and highest in Christianity.

Let us return, therefore, to the more typical "Christian Socialist" who retains at least some faint belief in the supernatural nature of our religion, though he is for ever readjusting her dogmatic attitude toward it at the dictation of the so-called higher critics. As with the dogmatic, so with the moral teaching of Our Lord, he seems never in the repose of certitude. His life is on quicksand, not on the rock.

This type of Christian Socialist will tell us that the early Church was socialistic, and that the Fathers inculcated pure Socialism. The same supposed fact is also alleged by Socialists who are not Christians, — sometimes by way of reproach against Christians who refuse to become Socialists, sometimes with a view to enlisting their sympathy.

Let us examine these supposed facts. And first as to the early Church.

The matter can be settled very simply. We have but to glance at the Acts to find that, not only was the practice of sharing goods confined to Jerusalem, but that it was not imposed upon any one. It was perfectly spontaneous, as the story of Ananias lets us see. Ananias was not punished for keeping his land ("Was it not still in thy power?" asks St. Peter); he was punished for telling a lie. To sell one's property and give the proceeds to the poor is still a course which the Church will encourage. But she will not, and she never did, enjoin it.

"But," urge the Christian Socialists, "the early Fathers of the Church taught Socialism." I reply that the early Fathers of the Church taught nothing of the kind. They taught the doctrine of their Master, and no other.

True, they say strong things about the duty of almsgiving. They speak out boldly in defence of the poor and suffering; they upbraid the rich for their cruelty and selfishness. But this has been done by Christian preachers in every age. I will undertake to find denunciations hardly less vigorous in the writings of Cardinal Manning or Bishop Ketteler, — nay, in those of Pope Leo

XIII and many another Roman pontiff. On this matter much has already been said. My point here is that you will not find in the writings of the Fathers any support for Socialism, — unless, indeed, you adopt the usual socialist device of wresting isolated sentences from their context and leaving out inconvenient phrases. Certain such hoary extracts are, as a matter of fact, passed on from one socialist writer to another. Let me give an instance or two.

We shall find two familiar quotations from the Fathers in the Fabian Tract which I have selected as a fair sample of Christian Socialist argument.

"Notice, for instance," says Mr. Dearmer, "how Tertullian appeals to the Socialism of the Church as a thing which can be taken for granted and which excites the wrath of the pagan world." He then quotes from the thirty-ninth chapter of that writer's Apology : —

"And they [the pagans] are angry with us for calling each other brethren. . . . The very thing which commonly puts an end to brotherhood among you [pagans], viz. family, property, is just that upon the community of which *our* brotherhood depends. And so we who are one in mind and soul, have no hesitation in sharing our possessions with each other."

But we have only to read the rest of the chapter in order to see that Tertullian is not talking about Socialism or anything like it. For he gives a detailed description of how this mutual help among the Christians was bestowed. He is careful to explain that each one gave to the common fund "when he wished and only if he wished and if he could" (*quum velit, et si modo velit, et si modo possit*). There was no compulsion (*Nemo compellitur sed sponte confert*). How on earth can this common Christian procedure be called Socialism? It is no more socialistic than the modern poor-rate, or the Sunday offertory. You must not, like Jules Blois, Anatole France, Sabatier, and Renan, read your own meaning into the lives of others. You must take the clear and obvious interpretation of their lives and writings.

Again, Mr. Dearmer writes (*l.c.*, p. 21, note) : —

"Prudhon's famous saying that 'property is robbery,' was anticipated 1600 years ago by St. Ambrose: 'Nature therefore created common right. Usurpation made private right' ('De Off.,' I, 28)."

This passage (like many similar ones to be found in the writings of Fathers and Schoolmen) is a positive pitfall for the Socialist who will not take the trouble to ascertain its meaning. "Nature" here, as so often, refers to the original dispensation of God, the order in which Adam was set before the Fall. Original sin shattered that order, and a new order had to be set up in its place. Private property was introduced, with God's sanction. St. Ambrose does not say that "usurpation" made private right. He says *usurpatio* made it. But the Latin word *usurpatio* means "frequent use and possession" no less than usurpation. Why does Mr. Dearmer ignore those other meanings of the word? St. Ambrose, while reminding the rich of their duties, explicitly vindicates the rights of private property. Evidently Mr. Dearmer has not read the sublimely eloquent treatise, "De Nabuthe Iezraelita," in which the holy Bishop speaks of Naboth the Jezrahelite and the vineyard of which King Achab wanted, at any cost, to get possession.

Once more, Socialists are fond of pointing to the Religious Orders, and claiming them as concrete examples of Socialism.

It is true that from some points of view a religious order may be called socialistic, or rather communistic. But it differs from Socialism, as commonly propounded, in several important particulars, with the result that it forms no precedent from which the modern Socialist may argue. The religious rule is based upon the religious vows, and is quite incapable of general application. Religious orders consist of men or women who *voluntarily* cut themselves off from family life, commercial pursuits, and the like, in order to devote themselves to the sanctification of themselves and their neighbours. Comparatively few make suitable candidates for a religious order. A long and severe training tests the capacity of each. Those who, after such training, voluntarily elect to join the order, find the life tolerable, not because it is naturally pleasant, but because it is supernaturally satisfying. Even these may sometimes discover that community life is, after all, too great a strain upon them, and may apply to the Holy See for a dispensation from their vows, and return once more to a life in which not so much is required of them.

True, there is much happiness in religious orders. Those who have had a glimpse of the life, and do not form their estimate of it from sensational paragraphs in the gutter press about "escaped nuns," often look wistfully and half enviously at the serene and satisfying atmosphere of a monastery or a convent, the delicate charity, the absence of sordid cares, the security, and the hope to be found there. That is all true. But the secret of this happiness does not lie in the economic arrangements of religious orders. It comes from their spirit of renunciation and loving service, without which life in religion would be unendurable. To attempt to force men who have not this spirit into the severe discipline of a monastic institution would be the most outrageous tyranny. It would be impossible of achievement. Nothing but strong ambition for God's glory, and zeal for the sanctification of souls; nothing but a community of spirit, and a tremendous personal love of Jesus Christ, could make it possible for religious communities to live together under the discipline of rule, bearing one another's burdens, and exercising mutual patience and charity.

We have seen therefore that the attempt to base Socialism on Christianity breaks down all along the line. It can only be made by perverting the plain sense of the Gospels, misinterpreting history, and ignoring the very marked characteristics of Socialism as an actual movement.

The position of the Catholic Church in the matter has been clear and consistent. She has watched the socialist movement in its growth (as she has watched every political and social movement in its growth for nineteen centuries), and she has seen it developing along lines which are incompatible with Christian beliefs and standards. She definitely tells her children to keep clear of it. Unlike the Bishop of Durham, she will not "venture to use the word apart from its historical associations" — for she knows well to what confusion of ideas such a twisting of terminology may lead. Eager as she is to take her part in social reform and to establish a Christian Democracy, she will not call her efforts by the name of Socialism or allow her children to join socialist bodies. For the name now stands for a definite movement with anti-Christian implications. It is idle to urge that the name denotes an economic theory only and that the movement might have proceeded on Christian lines. As a matter of fact it has not done so, and we must accept the facts as we find them. For the same reason the Church does not favour the use of the term "Christian Socialism," since it is productive of misunderstandings. Leo XIII ("Graves de Communi") observed that it had "justly fallen into desuetude." Let us define our terms and know what we are speaking about. Let us not forget that Christianity is one thing and Socialism another. The two systems work in opposite directions, and flow into different termini. Socialism makes for a Paradise beneath the moon, Christianity leads to a Heaven beyond the stars.

VII

SOCIALISM AND THE RIGHTS OF OWNERSHIP

SOCIETY rests upon a triple basis: private property is its material basis, the family is its natural basis, and religion its supernatural, its divine basis. We have already dealt with the question of the Family and Religion. We pointed out how Socialism, from the very nature of its constitution, is destructive of that sublime creation of God, the family. Socialists who are true to their cause, who with the founders of their cult, believe in the material conception of history, have no alternative but to tilt against the family as it has been understood since Christ first raised the sacred contract between man and woman into a divine Sacrament, thus making the unity and indissolubility of the marriage tie the very condition of the stability, unity, and harmony of the State.

Nor can Socialists who are trained efficiently in the ethics of their school tolerate religion. For them Socialism is their religion, and they will have none other. Indeed, they are careful to remind us that in Socialism there is no room for "starland religion," that the only religion in which the Socialist puts his trust is Democracy working for Democracy, and that the paradise for which he is striving is to be found not on a star map, but on the map of the world "right here." Having treated of the divine and the natural foundations on which Society depends for its unity, harmony, and stability, we will now proceed to speak of the material basis on which the State rests, property.

By private property I understand man's individual sovereignty over his acres, his home, his capital, his goods and chattels, his inheritance.

Among all civilized nations private ownership has been recognized, and in all civilized nations private ownership has been protected under the triple buckler of nature, justice, and religion. Without it society would lose its chief material support, and would slide away like a house undermined by a landslip.

Property, then, is a necessary basis of society, which could not exist without it. By it the family clings to the native soil as the tree to the earth by its roots. All nations have held it sacredly inviolable; all have clung to it, and we all to-day consider it so sacred as to protect it with our very lives; we consider it so just that any violation of it on our part would beget within us bitter remorse, which nothing but restitution could allay. Such being the case, how can any man contest a right so legitimate, so sacred to humanity? How in the full splendour of this twentieth-century civilization, with the sanction of all ages, of all schools, all magistrates, all governments, and all religions, can men who proclaim themselves civilized call in question the right of private productive property?

"Far from attacking private property, we ought to defend it. Far from suppressing it, we ought to extend it. Yes; let every man by his labour and thrift, his earnings and savings, economy and virtue, attain this sovereignty wherewith he is endowed by the right of private property. The ambition to possess and own something is a noble ambition, even though it extended only to a parcel of land which he must fructify by the sweat of his brow, and may transmit by inheritance to his children. To suppress private property because some may and have abused it is a stupid aberration. Is there anything that men may not and have not abused? Then suppress everything, even bread and meat, for there are some who dig their graves with their teeth. But to attempt to equalize all men, even the idler and lazy drone, the spendthrift, the drunkard, and the gambler, and cry out before that crowd, 'Property is theft!' this is not simply an error; it is a crime against society; it is shaking the material basis whereon society rests."

Now it is certain, it is a well-known and palpable fact proclaimed before all the world, that Socialism denies the right of private property. It blocks the way of Socialism. To employ the forcible language of Frederick Engels: "Three great obstacles block the way of Socialism, — private property, religion, and the present form of marriage." Socialism proposes to transfer private productive property from the individual to the Coöperative Commonwealth. It is a theory according to which people would be happier and better were the means of production thus transferred. In the concrete it is associated with other theories; but in the abstract "Socialism is a theory chiefly concerned with property, and nothing else."

There is a tendency amongst economic Liberals and Socialists alike to apply the name Socialism to any proposals for the public control of particular means of production. A Catholic who favours the nationalization of railways will be called a Socialist. A Conservative who suggests the municipalization of tramways is liable to be denounced by some of his colleagues as a Socialist. Indeed, any effort to improve the social condition of the people is sure to be called socialistic. When the Archbishop of Paris recently exerted his influence to protect the apprentices in the barbers' shops, his action was at once labelled Socialism by a section of the foreign press. An Employers' Liability Act is called Socialism by liberal Economists who disapprove of it. An Old Age Pensions Act is called Socialism by Socialists who welcome it.

Again, the immediate practical proposals of, let us say, a Catholic leader in Germany, may bear a striking resemblance to the immediate practical proposals of an English socialist leader. Yet the latter proposals are socialistic, while the former are not. There is a yawning chasm between them.

Let us endeavour to cut our way through this confused tangle and ascertain what Socialism really is, and how it differs from Catholic social reform.

We may take Socialists on both sides of the Atlantic and interrogate them. It will at once be seen that, although they may agree in their immediate programme, yet in principle, in ultimate aim, in their general outlook upon life, they differ profoundly and are in the sharpest antagonism.

R

The object of the Socialist is to get rid of private capital. He regards private capital as a mischievous thing, unjust in origin and criminal in results. His immediate proposals are merely the first steps towards its complete abolition. His ideal is the absolute transference of all the means of production to the State. He may not go so far as to say with Prudhon that "property is robbery," — though the saying I have often heard repeated in London Parks, in New York Avenues, and in miners' camps out West. He may not charge all capitalists of formal injustice, but he regards the system of private capitalism as essentially rotten. It must go — peaceably or violently. Private capital is an excrescence or a morbid growth in the history of man : or, at the very least, it is a phase which must be outgrown. It is not permanent. It is no essential part of the social structure. It answers to no deep-rooted and ineradicable demands of human nature.

The Catholic, on the other hand, if he really represents the sound Catholic tradition (for I do not deny that Catholics may be tinged with economic Liberalism or bitten with Socialism or — oftener still — in a state of muddle about the whole matter) — the Catholic, I say, who has grasped Catholic principles and has sufficient knowledge to apply them to modern conditions may be inclined to admit a large measure of socialization or municipalization of certain kinds of property. As we saw in our Conference on Socialism and the State, a wide increase of State action may be admitted and even demanded on Catholic principles.

But the Catholic *has* principles, and these principles are in direct contradiction to the doctrines of Socialism. The Catholic does *not* regard the private ownership of capital as something unnatural, or as a mere accident or excrescence. He regards it as something proper and normal to man : something which is necessary for social harmony and stability, and for the satisfying of man's deepest needs.

The Catholic will favour many measures which tend to limit the exercise of the right to own capital. But he does so, not in order to undermine that right, but in order to make it more secure and useful. Catholic principles which establish the right also prescribe, as we shall see, its limitations. The Catholic strives to check the abuses of private capital, the Socialist strives to abolish private capital altogether.

There is all the difference between these two points of view, and there will ultimately be all the difference between the kind of action which re-sults from them. The Catholic limits the right of ownership in order to make it more effective. The Socialist limits it in order to make it less so.

If a man has a troublesome tooth which causes him pain and upsets his health, he will go to a dentist and have it out. In the Middle Ages the extraction of teeth was not always remedial. It was sometimes punitive. A man might have his teeth drawn not because he was in pain, but in order that he might be put in pain. The ex-traction was not a step towards curing him, but a step towards killing him. He was regarded as an objectionable person to be weakened and brought low and struck at: not as a temporarily ailing person to be made strong and healthy. In both cases the operation was the same: the ex-traction of a tooth with a pair of pincers. But who will class the modern dentist with the medi-æval torturer? Their aims differ, and it is merely an accident that their actual procedure is, at one stage, alike. Give the torturer his way and he will not only pull out the man's teeth but take off his head. Give the dentist his desire, and he will save the tooth, and make it useful. If he cannot save it, he will replace it by another both useful and good.

Hence, before we can call a man who advocates high death duties, or a minimum wage, or old age pensions, a Socialist, we must ask a few questions. What is he after? What is his next proposal? How is this proposal related to his general views of human nature, of society, of government? Above all, what is his attitude towards private capital, — towards all private ownership?

Now, in this matter of private capital, the position of the Socialist is clear. He has his principle, and that principle is no mere extension of any principle admitted by Catholics. To quote Mr. Belloc : —

"The Principle of Socialism is that the means of production are morally the property not of individuals but of the State: that in the hands of individuals, however widely diffused, such property exploits the labour of others, and that such exploitation is wrong. No exceptions in practice destroy the validity of such a proposition. It is the prime conception which makes a Socialist what he is. The men who hold this doctrine fast, who see it clearly, and who attempt to act upon it and to convert others to it are the true Socialists. They are numerous, and what is more, they are the core of the whole socialist movement. It is their uncompromising dogma which gives it its vitality, for never could so vast a revolution be effected in human habit as Socialists in general pretend to effect, were there not ready to act for it men possessed of a definite and absolute creed." ("The Church and Socialism.")

Now against this socialist dogma the Catholic Church has set her face like a flint. She bans and condemns it. She herself may on occasion say very strong things to the capitalist, as her Divine Founder did before her. Early Fathers, the mediæval Doctors, have, like the Popes in all ages, insisted much upon the duties and responsibilities of wealth. But they have never, even amidst the utmost corruptions of capitalism, denied the right to own private capital. On the contrary, they have strongly upheld and vindicated it as being something inextricably bound up with human welfare, as a condition of normal civic freedom.

Attempts are often made by Socialists to enlist the Fathers of the Church in their cause. And there is no doubt that, taken out of the context, many passages from the Fathers of the Church, notably from the writings of St. Clement of Alexandria, St. Cyprian of Carthage, St. Gregory Nazianzen, St. Basil, St. Jerome, St. Ambrose, and St. Chrysostom smack of Socialism. But let us make no mistake about the point of view from which they speak. They were not teachers of economics, but of ethics. And for the most part they are dealing with questions not of justice, but of charity. Furthermore, many of the passages cited by Socialists occur in sermons, and a preacher, whose business it is to create an immediate impression; to make his listeners hear, understand, and feel; in a word to induce them to open their ears, to open their minds, and to open their hearts, and it may be, even to open their hands also, is allowed the use of language which in a writer on economics would be not only out of place, but wrong. Many of the Fathers, so triumphantly quoted by Socialists, were the sons of wealthy proprietors, and were themselves owners of private property and capital.

Later on I will endeavour to exhibit the strength of the Catholic argument even against those who will not admit the existence of revelation or supernatural guidance in the Catholic Church. I will undertake to show how strong is her case even from the mere historical standpoint.

But before doing so let me set out, first the teaching of the Catholic Church with regard to property, and secondly the mischievous doctrine of economic Liberalism upon the same subject —

a doctrine against which Socialism is in great part a natural protest and reaction.

According to Catholic teaching the right to own property is a natural right. This right is prior to society, and is based on the will of God. It is the will of God that men should own property and even productive property. Private capital is not the result of mere social convention; it is part of a natural and divine plan.

How is this divine character of the right of property established? In just the same way as the divine character of civil authority is established. That is to say, we may ascertain God's will in regard to it by examining human nature as it is revealed to us in history. Man has been set upon this earth in order to develop his material, intellectual, and spiritual capacities. With the *duty* of developing them goes the *right* of developing them. Now the Catholic Church maintains, and has ever maintained, that the possession of property (including capital) is a normal condition of this development. Man not only has a deep-rooted and natural desire to own property, but, as a rule, and speaking generally, if he is to develop according to the designs of God, he *must* own property.

Hence it is the desire of the Catholic Church

that as many men as possible should be proprietors: that they should not only procure the necessities of life from day to day, but also control such means of wealth as will ensure their permanent provision.

The justification for this doctrine has frequently been set forth by representative Catholic writers in all ages, and may here be briefly recalled.

Let us look first at the individual. We have in a previous Conference seen that the individual is something more than a cell in the social organism. True, he is a citizen with duties to society, but this does not exhaust his whole personality. He does not exist for the State: he is not wholly and in every particular subordinate to the State. As an individual, and as the member of a family, he has rights and duties which are independent of and prior to the State. He has an immortal soul directly created by God; he has a direct mission from God; and hence he has certain obligations and rights with which no State may interfere.

Taking man as an individual, therefore, we find that he has certain needs and requirements, and hence certain duties. He is bound to preserve his life, for that life is not his own; it is only lent him; it is God's. Hence he has the right to acquire, keep, control, and use whatever is necessary for the maintenance of that life.

This is a primary right, before which all other rights must give way. The Catholic Church teaches that a man who is in extreme need of the means of subsistence may take, from whatever source, what is necessary to keep him from actual starvation. A starving man who cannot otherwise obtain food may walk into a baker's shop and help himself to as much bread as is necessary to support life. He may do so openly or secretly, and in neither case will his action be one of theft. What is more, the baker has no right to prevent him, for the starving man is taking what he has a right to; to prevent his action would be an act of injustice. It may be illegal, and he would be taken up for doing so, but though it might be a deed against law, it would not be a sin against God.

This is the plain teaching of the Catholic Church enunciated by St. Thomas, and found in every Catholic textbook of moral theology. (II. II^{ae}, I. 66, a. 7.)

Man, then, has a right to live. He has a right to procure the necessities of life. He has a right to satisfy his absolute needs.

Now man's needs recur. He eats, and after a

while hunger returns. He requires shelter to-day and will require it to-morrow. To meet a recurring need he must procure permanent resources. Nature puts sources of supply within his reach: man must take them and control them. If they are not taken and controlled, they will not supply his permanent needs. He will not be secure, he will not be able to meet recurring needs, unless he can control the source of his supplies. Nature bids him provide for himself the means of production.

Moreover, we cannot bid a man limit his possessions to what is barely required for the satisfaction of the ordinary recurring needs. He is subject to accidents and to illness: he has to face the prospect of old age, and ought himself to make provision for it, and not depend on a pension. Hence, if he is to be put beyond the reach of destitution, he must acquire more than is necessary for the satisfaction of his immediate wants.

Again, man, endowed as he is with intellect and free will, is not a mere machine destined for a definite and limited measure of work and incapable of doing more. He has faculties which he can cultivate, potentialities which he can develop. And with this God-given power of self-development comes the right of self-development. Man must labour : but he does not exist merely that he may labour. He is no slave of his fellow-men or of society. He has not been sent into the world merely to contribute so many yards of cloth, or so many piles of bricks, or so many tons of coal, or so many yards of stone to the world's wealth. He has the right to cultivate his mind, to adorn his life intellectually, artistically, and morally. But this requires a certain economic independence. Here again we have the justification of the ownership of capital.

Now, when we turn from man as an individual to man as the father of a family, the justification becomes immeasurably more striking.

Of the institution of the family something has been said in a previous Conference. It has been shown that the family is a "natural" institution in the sense already explained ; that is to say, it is from God, and is no institution invented by man. But if we accept the institution of the family as something necessary and permanent, we encounter special reasons for regarding the institution of private capital as sharing in the necessity and permanence of the family. The point is insisted upon in the Encyclical "Rerum Novarum," of Pope Leo XIII.

"That right of property, therefore, which has been proved to belong naturally to individual persons must likewise belong to a man in his capacity of head of a family; nay, such a person must possess this right so much the more clearly in proportion as his position multiplies his duties. For it is a most sacred law of nature that a father should provide food and all necessaries for those whom he has begotten; and, similarly, nature dictates that a man's children, who carry on, so to speak, and continue his personality, should be by him provided with all that is needful to keep themselves honourably from want and misery amid the uncertainties of this mortal life. Now in no other way can a father effect this except by the ownership of lucrative property, which he can transmit to his children by inheritance. A family, no less than a State, is, as we have said, a true society, governed by a power within its sphere, that is to say, by the father. Provided, therefore, the limits, which are prescribed by the very purposes for which it exists, are not transgressed, the family has at least equal rights with the State in the choice and pursuit of the things needful to it for its preservation and its just liberty."

But here the Socialist will raise an objection. "All that you have proved so far," he will say, "is, that man has permanent wants, and that provision must be made for them. With this I agree:

but it is not an argument against Socialism. You have shown that there must be capital. I admit it. You have shown that the sources of supply must be controlled. I do not doubt it. But you have not yet justified *private* capital. You have not justified the private capitalist. My proposal is not to abolish capital but to transfer it, from the individual and from groups of individuals, to the community. My desire is not that the sources of supply should pass out of all control. My desire is that they should be controlled by the representatives of the people, in a word, by the whole Community."

"As for your arguments," the Socialist will continue, "they can be turned against you. You say that a man has a right to live, a right to satisfy his recurring needs, a right to develop his personality. Is he able to exercise that right in modern capitalistic society? Can our destitute poor be said to live? Are there not millions of men and women in America and England who live from hand to mouth, and are not certain of getting their next meal? As for development of personality and cultivation of the mind, how many can hope to dream of it?"

The Socialist will say: "Look at Pittsburg. Take those living there in Painter's Row — a cluster of houses near Painter's Steel Mill. What have you read about them? 'In one apartment a man, his wife and a baby, and two boarders slept in one room, and five boarders occupied two beds in an adjoining room. . . . Not one house in the entire settlement had any provision for supplying drinking water to its tenants. . . . They went to an old pump in the mill yard, — 360 steps from the farthest apartment, down seventy-five stairs. This town pump was the sole supply of drinking water within reach of ninety-one households comprising 568 persons. . . . Another row of one-family houses had a curious wooden chute arrangement on the back porches, down which waste water was poured that ran through open drains in the rear yard to the open drain between this row of houses and the next. . . . They carried other things besides waste water, — filth of every description was emptied down these chutes, for these six families, and three families below on the first floor, had no closet accommodations and were living like animals.'"

If no other facts than these were cited, the title of the chapter, "Low Wages and Standards," would be more than justified by the lowness of the wages and standards of Pittsburg, — "the city of a thousand millionnaires." But while the picture presented in Pittsburg is extreme, it is by no means exceptional. Similar descriptions, I am told, might be detailed of living conditions in the slumdoms of New York, the stockyards district of Chicago, the industrial towns of Pennsylvania, and the coal fields of West Virginia.

There is a reflex of these low standards of wages and of living, — a reflex on the children, a fact strikingly illustrated by the situation in Chicago. Two years ago the Chicago Board of Education investigated underfeeding among Chicago school children. The results of the investigation are thus reported : —

"Five thousand children who attend the schools of Chicago are habitually hungry. . . .

"I further report that 10,000 other children in the city — while not such extreme cases as the aforesaid — do not have sufficient nourishing food. . . .

"There are several thousand more children under six who are also underfed, and who are too young to attend school.

"The question of food is not the only question to be considered. Many children lack shoes and clothing. Many have no beds to sleep in. They cuddle together on hard floors. The majority of the indigent children live in damp, unclean, or overcrowded homes that lack proper ventilation and sanitation. Here, in the damp, ill-smelling basements, there is only one thing regarded as cheaper than rent — and that is the life of the child." ("Social Adjustment," p. 74.)

The objicient will continue, "No, the object of the socialist régime is to make man and woman secure, to let them feel that they are sure of food and shelter next week, and next year, and for the rest of their lives. Socialism will make it possible for men and women to develop their personalities, to cultivate their minds, to expand their sympathies and interests. Hence the arguments you have employed are arguments against Capitalism, but in favour of Socialism." ·

To this objection I reply as follows : —

If it could be proved that private capital is unable to supply the recurring needs of the human race and to secure the other results I have mentioned, then clearly my arguments would not tell in favour of private capital. And if at the same time it could be proved that Socialism is able to fulfil its promises, then, I admit, my arguments would tell in favour of Socialism.

But, as I shall proceed to show, private capital

s

is capable of supplying all the needs of the race, while Socialism is not. Hence the above arguments tell on behalf of Capitalism and against Socialism.

Even were Socialism able to perform what it promises, the foregoing argument would be valid, — not indeed against Socialism, but against propositions frequently laid down by Socialists.

Do not Socialists often declare that private capital is an essentially unjust thing? Now it must be remembered that a socialist régime has never yet been established. The world has had to get on all these thousands of years without Socialism, and meanwhile communities have had to live. Now the foregoing arguments have proved that *some* control of capital is necessary. Hence in the absence of public control it was absolutely necessary to have private control. But a necessity justifies itself: hence private Capitalism is vindicated from the charge of injustice.

"But at any rate," says the Socialist, "Capitalism has broken down now, and Socialism is the only system which can do the work that Capitalism can no longer do."

I answer that Capitalism has not broken down. I admit — with Leo XIII — that modern Capitalism is bristling with abuses. It has got out of hand. It requires drastic treatment. But Capitalism as a system does not stand condemned. Its abuses may be cured, as I shall indicate in my final Conference. Hence Capitalism is justified by the arguments which I have employed.

But what of Socialism? Could Socialism do the work for which Capitalism is declared to be incompetent and unequal? It could not. To prove this I will pass to another series of arguments which you may discover in the Encyclical "Rerum Novarum" of Leo XIII, and which may be traced back through St. Thomas of Aquin to Aristotle.

This line of argument is based, as Père Antoine points out, upon a very keen social psychology. It asserts that the private ownership of capital is required for the maintenance of social order, the securing of peace, and the progress of civilization. It appeals to certain primary facts about human nature which the Socialist too often overlooks. Let us consider one or two of these facts.

In the first place, we notice that men are more careful about their own property than they are about the property of others. A friend lately married writes to me, saying, that "wedded life makes one more careful of all goods and chattels than ever I thought could be possible." This admission may sound strange, but it is true and must be recognized. Could we transform the characters of men, a socialist régime would have something to be said in its favour. But Socialists seem to assume the improvement of character under their system without indicating any features of that system which are likely to produce it. Taking men as they are, we discover that they usually require the stimulus of private ownership before they will put forth their best work. Public administration is apt to be marked by wastefulness; municipal wastefulness has almost passed into a proverb. Give a man a share in a business, or in a piece of land and he will set all his wits to work discovering methods of economy of improvement, and of labour-saving devices, and so forth. Business firms everywhere recognize this. As a public official in a similar position he would not have the same spur to enterprise.

Now it is clear that disaster is in store for that society of which the members cease to exert themselves to the utmost in the development of their country's resources. I need not elaborate this point. Nations are no longer self-contained and self-sufficient. The markets of the world are confluent, and the life of a nation depends on its being able to maintain a very high level of industry, enterprise, and resourcefulness. Never be-

fore was the stimulus of private capital so necessary for national prosperity and security.

Again, the stimulus of private capital is required for another social reason. Not only is it
necessary as a direct condition of adequate production, but it is necessary on account of its reaction on character. The welfare of society rests
not only upon economic considerations, but upon
character. The object of civil society is not
only to produce wealth, but to develop character.
That the citizen should be industrious, sober,
manly, diligent, is to the advantage not only of the
citizen himself but of the society in which he lives.
These qualities not only help to produce wealth,
but they *are* wealth: they are among a nation's
most valuable assets.

Now these qualities are best sustained by a wide
distribution of private capital. I do not say that
they flourish particularly well under the present
capitalistic régime. On the contrary, they are at
present stunted and crippled. But the reason
of this is that the present capitalist régime is, as
Pope Leo XIII has told us, in an abnormal and
diseased condition. It is reeking with abuses.
But the abuses are not inseparable from Capitalism itself. They are the growth, like weeds, of
neglect, and have arisen from a betrayal of Chris-

tian principles. They can be cured by a return to Christian principles. They cannot be cured by Socialism.

They can be cured by a return to Catholic principles, because the Catholic doctrine of the rights of property is also a doctrine of the limitations and due use of property. Impress these principles upon society by means of legislation, private effort, and the influence of religion, and you will have a régime of property which will be free from current abuses, and will promote the good qualities which I have mentioned. Such a régime would heighten the sense of responsibility, and would lead men to pull themselves together, and to put forth their best work. Lay more stress on the family and the household, and on family capital, and you supply strong motives for persistent devoted effort.

Such results cannot be secured by Socialism. At first sight, indeed, Socialism would seem to make for a higher altruism. It is urged that just as society is a greater thing than the family, so it is more likely to call forth nobler and more unselfish effort. Socialists sometimes protest against the selfishness of family feeling, and claim that Socialism will widen men's horizon, and substitute unselfish work for society, in place of selfish competition on behalf of one's own family.

Does not such a claim show a strange ignorance of human nature? Man's powers are limited. In all cases he has to proceed from the less to the greater. He has to proceed from what is near and known to what is remote and unknown. He has to proceed from the particular to the universal. Citizenship is not a lesson that is easily learned. It must first be practised on a small scale in the family. A man must, as a rule, learn to administer his own private property before he can be trusted to administer public property. He must learn the lessons of honesty, industry, temperance, prudence, unselfishness, and these lessons are best learned in the administration of private capital. The Socialist may call this statement a paradox, but I believe it to be true. History points to it. Where do we find the trustworthy public men, the incorruptible, prudent, conscientious administrators, the painstaking legislators, the good citizens? We find them among those who have been trained in the administration of honestly acquired private capital, in the ordering of the family homestead. I do not refer to a class of men who to-day are piling up rapid fortunes by questionable means: for they violate Christian principles both in the acquisition and in the use of their wealth. They are "grafters." I refer to those who in the Christian spirit regard themselves as merely stewards of their possessions, and who in the administration of that wealth learn the lesson of social altruism.

Not so long ago I sent an urchin, who had passed through his parochial school, into the service of an English shipping merchant. He started as an errand boy. His Presbyterian employer called him into his office and asked him if I had given him any advice or directions to secure his climbing up in the business.

The boy answered that I had given "a whole lot" of advice, and that I had ended it by saying that he would find most of what I had said written up in tabloid form on the office door: "Push," which, when expanded, spelt out: be "Punctual, Upright, Sober, and Honest." The merchant was satisfied, and told the lad that if only he would put that advice into practice, he might most likely one day become a partner in that business. The boy is learning to become a steward of property.

Socialism would, I fear, be likely to breed a race of extravagant administrators. If no individuals owned capital, there would be no check on reckless spending. The salaried citizen would clamour for a higher salary without stopping to think whether the nation could afford to give it to him; he might help himself; he might help his friends;

he might create jobs for adventurers. He might abuse his position of trust and live on "graft."

And this leads me to another consideration.

It is a crime against society to weaken social stability. Our efforts must be to secure solidarity, to effect a unity of interest among the different classes of society, to weld all men together into a healthy and compact organism. We must not allow ourselves to be exposed to the danger of revolutions, as though we were a South American Republic.

Now social stability is undoubtedly fostered by the multiplication of capitalists in the country. The Socialist may object that the present capitalistic régime is unstable, and that we are in danger of revolutions. I admit it. But the reason is not because capitalists exist. The reason is because there are not enough capitalists. Capital is not sufficiently distributed. If we want to make society stable, we must give as many men as possible a stake in the country. The man who owns a home is not so likely to be a revolutionary as the lodger. The man who possesses a farm or a share in the industrial concern for which he works, is not so likely to welcome violent upheavals as the shifting wage-earner. The reason of this increased stability which follows the wide distribution of capital is no mere selfish one. Man does not strive for peace and counteract revolution merely because revolution might threaten his own property. But that property is the link which binds him to the nation. It brings his citizenship to a focus and gives it tangible shape. National peace and stability rest upon local peace and stability. The strength and virtue of society wells up like the sap in springtime from the land. Attach men to the land, give them a share in it, let them control it individually (either directly as small landowners or indirectly as shareholders in industrial concerns) and you give them character and stability. The weakness and peril of modern European nations lie not only in the "Industrial Workers of the World," but in the growing host of shifting proletarians. When Romans owned their farms Rome was strong. When they depended on public bread the nation was ripe for destruction.

How are we to account for the rush of all the nations of the earth to Canada and to the United States? In some districts you find a community made up of thirty-three nationalities and more. For the most part, among themselves, they talk, for a generation or two, the language of the land whence they came, they retain their ancient customs, have their own clubs, and guilds, and in some instances publish their own daily paper. Yet all these naturally conflicting elements become welded into one nationality, they become law-abiding American citizens, and rally to the star spangled banner with a readiness and loyalty beyond all praise. If you want the all-explanatory reason of this admirable catholicity of spirit, I need only remind you of the earth-pervading instinct in man for private and productive ownership. Just as the peasant in Ireland and the crofter in Scotland want to own their own bit of land, so all these immigrants, or whatever other name you may call them, swarm to the North American continent because they see the opportunity of becoming proprietors, capitalists.

In most of the Provinces of Canada, and of the States of America, people want to own their homes, or their homesteads, or their farms. They want to make their own businesses, and to become private owners of capital.

The same ambition is to be found among the aboriginal Indians. Every member of an Indian tribe is the owner of private property. As soon as the "papoose" appears, to it is given a horse, or a cow, or a sewing machine, or a dog, or a gun, or what not, so that by the time the young brave has attained manhood, he may find himself the owner of considerable property, all of which, in days gone by, would have been destroyed at his death. In a reservation in Montana every member of the Blackfeet was assigned by the government 320 acres of land. On the day on which the allotting agent arrived at the reservation a child was born. Needless to say, to that infant was given, no less than to the Chief, its own 320 acres.

I submit that grave objections may be brought against Socialism on the score that it would lead to evictions innumerable, that it would prejudice the healthy development of character, and threaten social stability. There are other serious economic difficulties against it, such as the enormous expense of public administration which it would entail, but these difficulties have frequently been set forth in books dealing with Socialism, and I need not consider them here.

I am concerned rather with specifically religious and moral objections to Socialism; and these I must develop further in the next Conference.

Among the many questions that have been sent me during the past month by Socialists, the following difficulties, as not unworthy of attention, I now propose to deal with briefly: —

(1) " Has a capitalist, or employer of labour, any claim in justice upon that surplus value remaining after working expenses of a business are paid, and the workmen's wages are paid and the employer himself is reasonably paid? Besides, is it not true that labour is the only source of value?" To the first part of this question I offer the following solution: In strict justice the surplus value referred to belongs to the employer, or capitalist, in the case; and it is for him to determine to what purpose to put it. Of course I presume that labour in the case referred to receives a living and not a sweated wage. The first duty of capital is to pay a decent remuneration for work done.

In spite of legislation against the sweater I am told that in the United States to-day "considerably more than two-thirds of the girls and women who work for a living in stores and factories are paid less than a living wage." "In Massachusetts 65 per cent of the candy workers, 40 per cent of the laundry workers, 40 per cent of cotton workers, get less than six dollars a week." With revelations such as these before us, there can be no question as to where *surplus values* ought to find their way. But given a living wage, then the residual portion of surplus value referred to in the objection may in strict justice be spent upon productive works, improved machinery, enlarged premises,—all of which indirectly benefit labour as well as capital. What might be best to do with this residual surplus value would be to create co-operative work, or better still, profit-sharing ventures, and best of all, copartnerships. Speaking on this subject as a set-off against the tactics of Socialists, a modern writer well says that:—

"We cannot pronounce that copartnership of itself, unaccompanied by some change of spirit on the part of rich people, would finally allay discontent. But, what is immeasurably important, it would start the reconstitution of society on lines that are sound, businesslike, evolutionary, instead of revolutionary," and found to be in operation in some American firms of standing. Who would not prefer it to the absorption of wealth by the State and the State officials? Who would not prefer it to the recurrence of devastating strikes?

"Where a workingman draws a share in the profits of industry, he knows that this share at least is not going to buy some rich man a new car. When times are good, he has tangible cause for rejoicing. When times are bad, he does not suffer alone. He has perpetually a strong interest against any event which injures the prosperity of his trade.

And, in his most rapacious mood, the method he must choose for increasing his share of good things cannot be a method that would involve his own property in ruin."

There are difficulties in the path, and it does not lead straight to a heaven upon earth. Like any other institution of society, it is unworkable without good-will. Like any other system, its success would depend on character.

"But we can claim that it offers to labour a stake in the country, a stake in organized society, and the least dangerous line along which to advance such further demands as labour may feel constrained to make."

As to the second part of the objection, namely, that to labour alone belongs the profits of a business. My only answer to this objection is, that on the face of it, it is as monstrous as it is absurd. Take a gramophone, a song, a novel, or any other commodity; their exchange values depend not only upon what mental and manual labor have been expended upon the article in question, but upon demand and supply, upon utility to the buyer, upon the rarity of the article, and upon its quality. A gramophone's value depends upon records, upon the make, upon the demand, upon the supply, upon the utility to the purchaser — and also upon the cost to the maker and the wages paid to the mechanic who turned it out.

(2) "Why should artists and poets, scientists and philosophers, be better paid for their work than blacksmiths, bricklayers, ploughmen, and carpenters? The former need no better food than the latter, and they are less necessary to the community. All should be paid alike."

This difficulty savours of a Fabian, who speaks of the artistic classes generally as "the high-priests of the modern Moloch." The artist, it is true, is not needed as much as the carpenter for the material well-being of the community. For the support of physical life the baker is more necessary than the painter. But there are other view-points besides those of the mere materialist. A skilled labourer who is making a frame for a portrait is not, I take it, troubled with the artistic temperament of the painter who fills in the canvas. Usually a joiner's work does not interfere with his sleep, health, and appetite. He is, as a rule, if not in rude health, at least normal. The artist certainly is not; he has to pay heavily for his genius. I myself have seen artists who, while engaged upon the canvas, have had more than once to leave their work, sick under the nervous strain caused by the artistic temperament. It is all very well to proclaim with the Fabian Shaw that an artist should be paid and fed no better than a ploughman, but the result of such treatment would be that you would have to get on with no better painters than signpost artists. Fine temperaments, as I once heard the late Laureate, Lord Tennyson, say, require fine things and fine treatment. Under a socialist régime there would be no room for the artist, his occupation would be gone. In a socialist atmosphere he could not live. He would fret to death like a swan in a duck pond.

(3) "Why should not the State be the sole proprietor of all the instruments of the production and the distribution of a country's wealth? Why should we not have State ownership, say, of all Railways, etc., as well as of all our Mails? If the Post-office is so successful, why should not other industries be equally so under State ownership?"

This difficulty is a very plausible one; but it is without legs on which to travel. Before citing the Post-office as their example, Socialists must prove, what they cannot, that to the Post-office is due the production of all the mails that are conveyed by that service. This they cannot do. Further, they must prove that the Post-office distributes the mail, which it certainly does not. It contracts with Railway and Steamship Com-

T

panies to carry what it has not produced and what it cannot distribute. As for State-owned railways, they compare very unfavourably with those owned by private companies. In Switzerland and Italy, in Australia and New Zealand, not to lengthen the list, have not Railway Systems owned and operated by the government been financial failures? They know nothing of the success of the Railway ventures in the United States. If Socialists urge that the State Railways of Germany, at any rate, are worked at a profit, I will remind them that they charge an average freight rate about double that of the United States. We are assured that if the Railways in the States were government property, worked on German lines, they would cost the country four million dollars a day more than they do at present. Finally, observe this, that the State-owned iron road, known as the Western Railway of France, has the reputation of being the worst managed in Europe. "Last year its loss was over thirteen millions of dollars." If we are to have good service, cheap rates, and high wages, we must also have competition, the outcome not of State but of private ownership.

(4) Another Socialist writes to ask me if there is any solution to the following difficulty. He tells me that this is a question proposed by the Hon.

Charles Russell, and is unanswerable. The question is this: "If it be lawful for the State to tax property at all, why is it not lawful for the State to take that property altogether? Practically it takes the lives of its soldier-citizens by sending them to the field of battle. If their lives may be taken, surely their property may be socialized." Before answering this difficulty I beg to state that I was present when Mr. Russell made the speech from which this question has been borrowed. In that speech Mr. Russell declared more than once that he was no Socialist. It is a libel upon him to say that he has identified himself with socialist doctrine. The questions which in that speech he proposed were uttered with the intention of eliciting the opinions of others rather than of expressing his own. Mr. Russell is too well acquainted with the Christian idea of the State and of its functions ever to have put forth as his own the sentiment expressed in the objection with which I now propose to deal.

The State, let it be remembered, is an institution set up by man not to appropriate but to protect him and his property, not therefore to absorb but to assist him by giving him the opportunity of doing what he ought to do, but what he cannot do without the protection and assistance of the State. It is the function of the State to look to the well-being of all its citizens, to prevent the clash of individual interests, and to provide as far as may be for the temporal welfare of the community as a whole. Clearly this cannot be done without legitimate taxation of property. Not even the State can carry on its various works without wage-paying, etc. How, let me ask, is the State to be financed except by a well-ordered system of taxation? What become of the highways, of the police and magistracy, of the Navy and Army, if the treasury is depleted? Cut off the supplies coming from taxation and you paralyze the action of the State. We tax property to protect and assist it, not to appropriate and assimilate it. If we send our armies into battle, it is not that they may be shot down, but that they may defend our homes and our property, and protect our country from becoming the spoil of our enemies. The analogy drawn between the army and the socialization of private property will not work.

Let me close this series of difficulties by an extract from Pope Leo's Encyclical on the Condition of the Working Classes. He writes that: "The foremost duty of the Rulers of the State should be to make sure that the laws and institutions, the general character and administration of the Commonwealth, shall be such as of themselves to realize public well-being and private prosperity. This is the proper scope of wise statesmanship and the work of the heads of the State."

May these wise words of the sovereign Pontiff sink into our hearts and draw forth from them the spirit of Christian citizenship which recognizes the duties no less than the rights of private ownership.

VIII

SOCIALISM AND THE DUTIES OF OWNERSHIP

ON my arrival in the United States, the very first number of the *International Socialist Review* which came my way was decked out in a brilliantly coloured cover-design which I will attempt to describe. The picture was cleverly drawn and was intended to symbolize as well as to synopsize the teaching of Socialism.

Imagine, then, a pyramidal structure, supported on the shoulders of men, women, and children, who, bowed and groaning under the weight crushing out their lives, are attempting feebly to cry out: "We work for all;" "We feed all."

On the first stage above the base of this pyramid thus supported by the proletariat is depicted a scene in which capitalists and other employers of labour are having a good time, — feasting, carousing, and loitering in luxury and idleness. The motto emblazoned across this *mise en scène* is significant: "We eat for you."

On the stage immediately above this we are shown naval and military forces clad in the garb of battle, standing behind their guns and awaiting the order to fire upon any section of the community which should dare to revolt against the tyranny of capital. The motto inscribed across this picture is: "We shoot at you." On the next platform above this tragic scene there stand out priests, and an altar with book and candles and censer, all of which is to be interpreted by the text written across the floor: "We fool you." Next to this comes the top stage, on which we recognize kaisers and kings, with other potentates, who owe their position to such servile creatures as the capitalist and the priest of the Catholic Church. On the apex of this wicked pyramidal frontispiece stands the money-bag, "the God and Ruler of all."

We all know that there is nothing so telling in a picture gallery as the canvas with a story. To it more particularly the wage-earner is drawn. The editors of the *I. S. R.*, then, have made use of this time-famed method of teaching in order to convey their own diabolical doctrines of class hatred to the breadwinner, who is told that property is robbery, and that he, with his fellows, is being exploited, crushed, and ground to the dust, not only by capitalists, but even still more by the Church, whose proud boast it is that it is the direct and immediate pillar support of law, order, and authority in the State.

Capitalist exploitation, we are assured by Victor Berger, is better than Roman Catholic exploitation. What blocks the way of Socialism is Catholicism.

When lecturing in the Eldorado district, I visited a prison, where I came across an English Socialist serving his time for having "pinched" nuggets. He had been suspected, so, impressions having been first of all taken, a certain number of nuggets were hidden away in the claim where he was mining as a wage-worker.

The missing gold treasures were discovered in his mouth and on his person. He was forced to disgorge them and to pay the penalty of two years in the penitentiary. He had socialist doctrine and training to thank for being in jail. He protested that he had only taken his own, and less than his share. In fact, he had reclaimed what had been stolen from him and his by that robber class called private property owners.

The Mounted Police had done the prisoner a good service, for when I saw him the second time, he asked me to write home to Whitechapel and tell his wife that he had "quit the comrade gang," and he added: "You will be sure, Father, to tell them at home that I have no more use in future for Socialists nor for rattlesnakes. When I come out," he continued, "there's not a bulldog but I'll look in the eye. I'll have a shack of my own, and I'll work for my own, and when I am laid in the ground I'll have a grave of my own. It's property as makes the man, and no two ways about it."

We have seen in the previous Conference that man as an individual and as the father of a family has a right to make provision for his permanent needs, and that the normal and natural way of doing so is by acquiring possession of some part of those sources of supply with which nature has so wonderfully and plentifully provided the human race. This method of providing for human wants has been a method actually practised among all peoples, and in all ages. On the great Western continent in this New World this scheme of things still obtains.

But now comes the Socialist who advocates what he considers to be a more effective method, namely, the transfer of all the means of production to the community, to be administered by the civil authority.

We have already seen in our second Conference that the State is a natural institution with certain well-defined rights and duties which are restricted by prior claims and duties of the individual and the family. Hence we may say at once that Socialism is not a natural or normal solution. It goes counter to the purpose for which the State was instituted through man by God. Under Socialism State action becomes a substitute for individual action, rather than supplementary to it. The individual, as has already been shown, becomes swallowed up in the State. This is an inversion of the natural order.

Hence the presumption is in favour of private capitalism, which I have shown to be a natural arrangement. That arrangement could be legitimately upset only on the supposition that it had ceased to be capable of fulfilling its purpose. Socialism to be justified would have first of all to prove there was no alternative.

Now I shall point out in my last Conference that the present capitalistic system is capable of being reformed. Its abuses may be corrected. They are not inherent in the system. Hence this is the direction in which we should bend our efforts. This would remain true even were Socialism to prevail. For even were Socialism to prevail it would not cease to be unnatural.

Socialism is unnatural. This is a point which I wish to develop in this chapter. It is a point which will involve a further consideration of the Catholic doctrine about property, which I have already shown to be in accordance with normal and healthy human instincts.

Socialism would thwart and cripple certain natural desires and aspirations in man which the Catholic Church seeks to foster and develop. In the first place, it would destroy man's freedom.

The Socialist will resent this statement. He will declare that men and women are not free at present; that they are entangled in the wheels of a cruel industrial system, and that Socialism alone can and will set them free.

But I repeat that under Socialism men and women would not be free. Even though they had plenty to eat and drink, and wherewith to be clothed, and wherein to be sheltered, they would not be free. They would not be free because they would not be masters of their own lives, nor would they be able to order their lives as they chose. I admit that the power of ordering their lives as they choose is to-day, owing to the abuses of the present system, very limited. But under Socialism the power would not exist at all. There would be no room for self-determining action. There would be one master, one general manager. In all the details of work and recreation, at every turn and moment of his life, a man would find his activities directed by the public authority. He could not stand out or strike against his employer, for his employer would be the State. He could not buy anything, or read anything, or eat anything, or do anything, unless the State chose to let him. He would have as much freedom only as a cog in a piece of machinery, as a nerve centre in a living organism.

Let it not be said that since the man himself would be a part of the State he would exercise control over public administration. What sort of control, I ask, would it be? Would it be comparable to the immediate control which a man has over his own actions and destiny? By no means. Man's personal influence over public administration would be as a drop in the ocean. It would be far from satisfying that desire to control his own life to which every healthy-minded man clings. It would certainly not enable us to say of a man that he was free.

Again, Socialism would give absolutely no scope

to that desire to own productive property which is natural to man, and which is particularly noticeable in the case of the Western races.

Again, the Socialist objects that this desire can only be gratified by a few under the present system. To this I reply that this is due to the abuses that have crept into the system, and not to the system itself. Because few only can satisfy that desire to-day, is that a reason for making it impossible for any one at all to satisfy it?

I believe that this desire to own productive property is a strong, healthy, and natural desire. It is something much more solid than a mere desire to possess the comforts and conveniences of life. Neither is it a mere desire to exploit the labour of others. It is a desire to protect one's freedom, to secure one's independence, to preserve one's personal respect, to assert one's manhood.

This last point has been well developed by Mr. Belloc in a paper entitled *An Examination of Socialism:* —

"Where few own, the mass who do not own at all are under a perpetual necessity to abase themselves in a number of little details. That is why industrial societies fight so badly compared with societies of peasant proprietors. The mass of the population gets trained to the sacrifice of honour;

it gets used to being ordered about by the capitalist, and partially loses its manhood. If there were but one capitalist, the State, this evil would certainly be exaggerated. Men would necessarily have lost all power of expression for the sentiment known as personal honour; they would have one absolute master, all forms of personal seclusion from whom would be impossible. This, when it is stated in the midst of modern evils, appears a very small point; but those who have passed by compulsion from a higher to a lower standard of personal honour can testify how vital a point is that honour in the scheme of human happiness."

And finally we may take higher ground and consider not merely the economic disadvantages of Socialism, or its failure to satisfy human needs, but its inherent injustice.

A government for the public good may place considerable limitations on the acquisition and control and use of property. But for the government to seek to take all productive property away from its owners must necessarily be an act of rank injustice. It could only be justified by absolute necessity, and that necessity does not and cannot exist.

As Pope Leo XIII says in the Encyclical: —

"When man thus turns the activity of his mind

and the strength of his body towards procuring the fruits of nature, by such acts he makes his own that portion of nature's field which he cultivates — that portion on which he leaves, as it were, the impress of his individuality; and it cannot but be just that he should possess that portion as his own, and have a right to hold it without any one being justified in violating that right."

Man is a free being and his whole nature rebels against the injustice of depriving him of what by the legitimate exercise of his faculties he has made his own. Whether what he has made be itself productive or not makes no difference. His sentiment of justice is outraged by its deprivation, save where such confiscation is absolutely necessary for the well-being and safety of the community.

Now in order to grasp the full significance of the Catholic doctrine of private capital we must examine at some length what the Church has to say about the acquisition of property and the limitations of property. In this way, so it seems to me, we shall put ourselves in an impregnable position against the specious arguments of the Socialist.

All men, according to the teaching of the Catholic Church, have the right to own capital. They have the right to own capital for the excellent reason that they are men. But to possess the right to own capital is not the same as actually to possess it. All men because they are men have an equal right to own capital; but they have not all an equal right to own the same capital. The right which we all equally possess may be called an abstract right. It does not beget or bequeath to us the property. We have to make the abstract right concrete, to exercise it, before we can acquire the property.

I remember a parish priest in Ireland saying to his poverty-stricken flock in Mayo, during Lent: "My brethren, the Bishop of the Diocese gives you permission to eat meat three times a week. But the Lord knows where ye'll get it from."

It is much the same with the right of property. By virtue of it we may acquire and hold property — supposing that we can get it.

It might seem as though a vague, shadowy right of this sort were of very little practical moment. But this is not the case. As a matter of fact, the abstract right of possessing private capital is bitterly attacked in these days; and we have to vindicate the great basic principles upon which the true Catholic doctrine of property rests. Before proving that *this* man has a right to *this* property, I must prove that man in general has a natural right to own property in general. And this I have just attempted to do.

But it is no less important to go on to show how this right of ownership may be made concrete. The right would indeed be useless if it could not be exercised. God, who has given us the right, has also given us legitimate methods of employing that right and realizing it.

Now there are certain well-recognized methods by which property may legitimately and justly come into a man's possession. I may be given a farm, or I may be bequeathed a farm, or I may buy a farm in the market. In each case the farm becomes my property.

But a further question will arise. The man who sold or gave me the farm must have owned it himself before he could transfer it to me. What was his title of ownership? If I answer that it was purchase or gift, I am driven further and further back, until I come to the first person who owned the farm, the original owner. What claim had the first owner to acquire it? In other words, I want to know the ultimate justification and title of ownership. Sale and gift and other methods by which property changes hands are derived and secondary titles. To justify them I must justify the action of the man who was the first occupier

u

of the land. If the first proprietor had not just title to the land, subsequent transference cannot be justified. And although practically all acquisition of property is nowadays of this derived or secondary character, yet we must make sure of our claims by examining the original title deeds.

Now the Catholic Church teaches that under certain recognized conditions a man may acquire property simply by occupying it.

What are these conditions? In the first place, the article in question (whether land or anything else) must not have been occupied by any one else. It must be *res nullius.* Secondly, the act of occupying it must be definite and effective and manifested by some external sign. A man cannot land on a newly discovered continent and say with a sweep of his arm, "In my own name I proclaim all this continent to be mine." He must mark out the ground he intends to occupy by some distinct sign. If he cultivates the land or puts his labour into it, his title becomes still more clear. But this is not necessary. It is enough that he should be able to supply juridical proof that he has in reality occupied it.

Observe well that the mere fact of occupation does not in itself constitute the right to occupy it.

I must have the right to occupy a thing before I occupy it, otherwise I have no title to the occupation. My act of occupation is merely a juridical fact which turns a latent right into an actual right, an indefinite one into a definite one. By my act of occupation, my natural right, given me by God, receives its final determination; it is put into exercise.

How do I show that mere occupation of a thing is sufficient determination of my natural right to own property?

I show it first by appealing to universal practice. In all ages such an act of occupation has been recognized as conferring a just title to ownership. Study the methods by which in the States and in Canada men have acquired property, and you will find that the method I refer to obtains.

Again, there must be some method by which man's right to acquire and hold property can be exercised. It would be absurd to suppose that all men possess a right which no man can enjoy. But no other method of exercising this right can be suggested; for the supposition that labour alone confers this right is quite untenable. (Cf. Cathrein, "Moral Phil.," n. 378.) Hence, we are driven to conclude that the recognized and traditional method of acquiring property in the first instance is in fact the only adequate and satisfactory method.

Note that this method violates no man's rights; for occupation is only a valid title in the case of what is previously unoccupied. By occupying a piece of land I am not wronging Peter and John, who have not occupied it before me. I am not wronging the community, for, as we have seen, private ownership is required for social welfare. I am not wronging the State, for the State is not the owner of all property. I am merely exercising a right which I hold from nature, and exercising it in a natural way.

Of course my action in so doing may be limited by other considerations. I cannot occupy a whole district if such occupation will result in misery for the rest of the community. To this point I will return later when dealing with the limitations to the right of ownership. At present I am merely defending the traditional method of exercising that right.

Let me here dispose of an objection which was raised and refuted more than two thousand years ago, but has been popularized by the late Henry George. ("Progress and Poverty," pp. 212–224.)

"Has the first comer at a banquet the right to

turn back all the chairs and claim that none of the other guests shall partake of the food provided, except as they make terms with him? Does the first man who presents a ticket at the door of a theatre and passes in, acquire by his priority the right to shut the doors and have the performance go on for him alone?"

"In like manner," contends Henry George, "our rights to take and possess cannot be exclusive."

St. Thomas answers this very objection. (II. II^{ae}, Q. 66, a. 2.) He points out that the man who came first into the theatre would do no wrong by preparing the way for others. He would only do wrong if he prevented others from enjoying the show. "And similarly a rich man does no wrong if, being the first to take possession of what was to begin with common property, he lets others also have the benefit of it; but he sins if he excludes others from the use of it in their necessity."

Observe that St. Thomas does not regard the possession of private capital as a keeping out of other people from the use of the good things of the earth. On the contrary, he regards it as a natural and divinely sanctioned arrangement which is for the advantage of society, and tends to bring those good things within the reach of all. The owner of capital "prepares the way " for others, he does not exclude them. He renders service to the community. His right of property carries with it certain social obligations.

The doctrine of the Church on this matter is so important that I must be allowed to set it forth in some detail. If we do not grasp it, we shall fall into the mistakes made by socialist writers who claim to find Socialism in St. Thomas and the Fathers.

In the first instance we must bear in mind the distinction between the *control* of property, and the *use* and *enjoyment* of property. Socialists admit the distinction, but seem incapable of recognizing it when it appears in the writings of a Catholic author.

I may have the control of a thing without being allowed the use of it. And I may have the use of a thing without having the control of it. Let me illustrate my meaning.

In a family the children have the use of their clothing, but not the control of it. The parents have the control, but not the use of it. My right to enjoy the use of a public park or library gives me no right to manage and control it. The Baths Committee have the control of the women's baths, but not the use of them. The Prisons'

Commissioners have the control of the convict's cell, but not the use and enjoyment of it. I may have the use of train service, but not the control of it. I may have the control of a baby-cart, but not the use of it.

Now this distinction must be constantly kept in mind if we are to understand the Catholic doctrine of the right of property. The Church says certain things about the control of property. She says certain other things about the use and enjoyment of it. If we confuse the two, we shall make her talk Socialism, which is the last thing she wants to do.

What, then, does the Church say about the *control* of property? She says that individuals and families may very properly possess such control. Private control is not only licit, it is as we have seen, socially necessary. The right to possess private capital is exclusive, and perpetual, and transmissible. A man does not lose his right to his own property even though he makes bad use of such right.

But when the Church speaks of the *use* of property, she uses very different language. The right to control property is an exclusive right. The right to use property, however, is of a different nature. As far as the use of things goes, says St.

Thomas, "man should not consider his outward possessions as his own, but as common to all, so as to share them without hesitation when others are in need." Pope Leo XIII, in his Encyclical, "Rerum Novarum," quotes these very words, prefacing them by the significant expression, "The Church replies without hesitation in the words of the same holy Doctor."

The Catholic doctrine as to the use of property is very clear and very definite, very strong and very striking. It is poles asunder from the egotistical view of the use of property which unfortunately prevails in our capitalistic society, and about which I shall say something presently. The Catholic Church regards property not as a mere means to selfish enjoyment, but as a public trust. The possessor of capital is a steward, exercising exclusive control of something from the use of which he must not exclude others in their need.

In other words, property, according to Catholic teaching, has a definite social function. A Catholic would not indeed say that private ownership *is* a social function; for this might imply that the right is derived from society and that owners are merely the delegates and employees of society. This is not the case. The right is a natural right and springs from the right to live a normal, social life possessed by every individual. But, nevertheless, the Church affirms that ownership has a social rôle, social duties, a social function.

There can be no doubt that had the Catholic doctrine as to the use of property been generally recognized and acted upon, the social problem could never have reached its present critical stage. For the Church bans and denounces that selfish view of property which has led to the present disorganization of society. And in this, her teaching, she has been unfaltering and uniform, from the time when Christ threatened those who misused their right to property with eternal damnation, down to the day when Pope Leo XIII strove to recall modern Capitalism to a sense of its obligations.

Wealth is a trust. Rich men are stewards. They must give of their superfluities to those who need them. They are not left free in the matter. A rigorous obligation is imposed upon them.

Observe the splendid consistency of the Catholic doctrine. The very same principle which establishes the right of private property also establishes its limitations. The doctrine is based upon God's law, it secures God's rights, it corresponds to the highest human sentiments of mutual love and of social solidarity. It prevents the goods of the earth from becoming the prey of the selfish few. It opens out to all men the enjoyment of the good things of the earth. If strictly observed, it mitigates the lot of the poor, while at the same time it preserves the social order by upholding the right of private control. It recognizes the element of truth in the two exaggerated theories of absolute ownership and of Socialism. It unites private control with common use.

The Catholic theory is the only theory which is proof against the criticism of Socialists. Those who deny that the use of property is common have no answer to give when the Socialist points to the awful contrast which at present exists between luxurious and destitute classes. The Catholic, like the Socialist, denounces the modern evils of Capitalism; but he would abolish these evils not by making control public but by making use common; by making it obligatory in charity on the rich to give of their abundance to those who are in need of material help.

It would take us too long to examine in detail the magnificent system of social obligations which the Catholic Church has built up. That system has its firm roots in theology and philosophy, it satisfies every requirement of justice and charity, it takes account of man both as an individual and as a member of society. Let me briefly enumerate some of its features.

Of the obligation to relieve those in extreme necessity I have already spoken. Other obligations also exist; that, for instance, of paying a just wage to servants and employees. This is an obligation of strict justice. The salary given must be sufficient to support the wage-earner. If, under the pressure of necessity, a workingman accepts less than a living wage, the Church declares that the contract is not only harsh and cruel but also invalid and unjust. The Church will not listen to those who say that such contracts are merely a private matter between master and man, and that if the workman accepts bad conditions because he cannot get better ones, yet he freely contracts. Pope Leo XIII, in the Encyclical so often quoted, points out that the man in such a case is not really free. He is the victim of force and fraud.

There are other duties of strict justice which are too often overlooked. Too many forget that to put off paying debts to tradesmen is a gross act of injustice persistently denounced by the Church.

But let us pass from duties of justice to duties of charity. And let me point out that the obligation may be as grave in one case as in the other.

The Catholic notion of charity is often misunderstood, and some seem to imagine that because a duty is a "duty of charity," it may be neglected. The difference between justice and charity is important, and has important consequences, especially as regards the obligation of restitution. But this does not mean that charity is optional. Christ threatens with eternal punishment those who neglect to practise it.

What, then, are the "duties of charity" connected with ownership? Here are some of them: —

1. There is the grave obligation to help the poor. This is an absolute command. The teaching of the Church on this point has been constant. Pope Leo XIII writes thus: —

"True, no one is commanded to distribute to others that which is required for his own needs and those of his household; nor to give away what is reasonably required to keep up becomingly his condition in life; 'for no one ought to live other than becomingly.' But when what necessity demands has been supplied, and one's standing fairly taken thought for, it becomes a duty to give to the indigent out of what remains over. Of that which remaineth, give alms. It is a duty, not of justice (save in extreme cases), but of

Christian charity — a duty not enforced by human law. But the laws and judgments of men must yield place to the laws and judgments of Christ, the true God, Who in many ways urges on His followers the practice of almsgiving — '*It is more blessed to give than to receive;*' and Who will count a kindness done or refused to the poor as done or refused to Himself. '*As long as you did it to one of My least brethren, you did it to Me.*' To sum up, then, what has been said: Whoever has received from the divine bounty a large share of temporal blessings, whether they be external and corporeal, or gifts of the mind, has received them for the purpose of using them for the perfecting of his own nature, and, at the same time, that he may employ them, as the steward of God's Providence, for the benefit of others. 'He that hath a talent,' says St. Gregory the Great, 'let him see that he hide it not; he that hath abundance, let him quicken himself to mercy and generosity; he that hath art and skill, let him do his best to share the use and the utility thereof with his neighbour.' "

Note that this duty being one of charity, the poor have not a right of strict justice to the superfluous wealth of the rich. They have no legal claim to it, as they have to just wages or debts. But the rich are nevertheless absolutely bound in charity to give it.

2. This duty of charity is specially urgent in the case of those more closely connected with us by natural or social ties. The employer has special duties of charity towards his employed, the master to his servants, the landowner to his tenants. There is more than a mere cash nexus between them: there is a social bond, and it involves its obligations.

3. We may add various other obligations equally certain, sacred, and strict which may be called duties of "natural equity." [1]

Under this head may be enumerated the following duties which attach to property: —

1. To respect the dignity of the poor and of the working classes.

2. To enable employees to fulfil their duties as husbands, fathers, citizens, and Christians.

3. To avoid imposing work which is beyond the strength of workers or unsuited to their age or sex.

4. To compensate employees for accidents. This becomes a matter of strict justice when the accident is due to the employer's fault.

---

[1] Some prefer the term "social justice." But this expression is vague and may easily lead to confusion.

5. To safeguard the innocence of children and the honour of women.[1]

We might add yet other duties which press upon the employer: those, for instance, of giving good example, of supporting religion, of promoting the political and social education of their people and the material prosperity of the district, and also of cultivating that cordial personal contact with their employees which is so necessary for social peace and well-being. Absenteeism is not blessed by the Catholic Church.

And finally, what is the duty of the State towards the right of property?

The State must recognize the right, respect it, protect it. The State may also be called upon to regulate and limit its use. I have already explained the purpose and aim of civil authority. That purpose and aim regulates the limits of civil interference. When public rights conflict with private, the latter must give way: and in this matter the State is the arbiter. Yet as Père Antoine points out, it may not be arbitrary in its arbitration. Its right to limit the use of property springs from and is limited by its incontes-

---

[1] (These duties are insisted upon in the Pope's Encyclical and have been explained at length by the Abbé Garriguet in his work, "Régime de la Propriété.")

table right to existence and self-preservation, by its right "to furnish citizens, by means of social organization, with the possibility of developing, by private initiative, their personal well-being."

The State has no direct and immediate power over private property, but it may reconcile its mode of acquisition and its use with the common good. The right of the State is a power of jurisdiction falling directly on individuals and only indirectly on property.

This principle will be found worked out in detail by Père Antoine in his excellent work just referred to. He shows how the State should promote the stability of the family by making wise laws of inheritance, how it should frame legislation which will give a special measure of protection to the working classes, and how it should facilitate division of landed property, counteract its abnormal accumulation in a few hands, and give the fullest protection to all healthy forms of association.

It will be seen, then, that the right to own property is, in the eyes of the Catholic Church, hedged about with very serious obligations, and that the State must coöperate in enforcing them. If these obligations were realized and practised, we should be halfway to a solution of our social problems. But it is to be feared that these obligations are often overlooked even by Catholic employers. The truth is that the teaching of the Church in these matters has been obscured by the anti-Catholic wave of economic Liberalism which swept over Europe during the last century, but which is at last beginning to ebb. The theory of the "absolute right of property," which regards property as existing merely for the benefit of the owner, is an exaggeration no less mischievous than the opposite exaggeration which it has produced by a natural reaction and which forms the basis of Socialism.

Let me here summarize the excellent criticism of the false theory which is to be found in the treatise of Abbé Garriguet.

1. The Theory is anti-Christian, for it is based on egoism. Christianity says we are all children of one Father, and have mutual duties.

2. The Theory is anti-Natural. It is, as Bishop Ketteler says, a crime against nature, because it uses for selfish gratification what God has intended for the service of all : and also because it stifles noble sentiments, and breeds callousness, indifference, and insensibility to human suffering.

3. The Theory has never been admitted by the

x

Church. The Popes, as civil rulers, persistently obliged the great landowners during seven centuries to provide the labourers with small holdings, even at considerable loss to themselves. If a landowner refused to cultivate his own land, any person whatever might occupy and cultivate (either free of charge or on payment of a small rent in kind) one-third of the land thus left uncultivated. The owner who attempted to evict such a tenant was heavily fined. Church land came under this provision.

4. The Theory has never been admitted in practice by any government. The State has always claimed to impose limits to the use of private property whenever the public welfare has required it. Bear in mind that the only effective way of refuting the socialist position is by the statement of the Catholic position. When we grasp the teaching of the Church with regard to the right of property, its nature and origin, its limitations and consequences, we see that it provides a remedy for the abuses against which Socialism rightly protests, while at the same time it avoids the errors and exaggerations the socialistic solution involves.

The essence of Socialism is that all the means of production should be transferred to the community. We have seen that such a transference would be contrary both to justice and to natural law.

Now some of my readers may endeavour to sweep away the whole of the foregoing argument by denying the basis upon which it rests. They may refuse to allow that we have any knowledge of God's will in the matter, or indeed of His very existence. They may take their stand upon a materialistic theory of evolution. They may refuse to believe in a supernatural order. They may decline to regard the Catholic Church as the authoritative exponent of the divine will.

I cannot pursue them on to this wider ground within the limits of this course of Conferences. But let me invite them to reflect upon an undeniable historical fact.

They do not admit that the Church speaks with divine authority. But they are bound to admit that the Church speaks with the very highest human authority. They deny that the Church speaks with the wisdom of God. They cannot deny that the Church speaks with the accumulated wisdom of men. The Church, at the very least, is the greatest expert to be found on the face of the earth in human nature and human history.

No man, no body of men, no institution, can rival

her in experience and insight. She has been studying the history of men and nations for nearly two thousand years. Nay, she has taken the leading part in the making of that history. She is the greatest fact in that history. She has been in the closest contact with all nations: she has watched them rise and fall. She is always teaching; she is always learning. She is always making use of that learning. She is concerned with every aspect of human life. She deals with man in a far more intimate way than any government can do or wants to do. She draws out his secrets, she learns his needs, she divines his aspirations, she marks his limitations, she estimates his possibilities, she lifts up his ambitions. All this must be admitted by the serious student of history.

Hence the mere human authority of the Church is of incalculable weight. She knows what is in man. She knows what faith inspires him, what motives actuate him, what circumstances affect him. She knows what is essential and normal to him, and what is merely accidental and transient. And when she says that the possession of private capital is essential to the welfare both of the individual and of society, we may be sure she is right.

She warns us against transferring all capital to the control of governments. She urges us to procure its wide and equitable distribution among citizens. She declares that only thus can we ensure social stability, peace, and prosperity; only thus can we develop man's highest possibilities. She declares that the instinct to own capital is a part of our human outfit, an ineradicable instinct which we cannot overlook with impunity. That is a message which no man can afford to disregard.

In conclusion, let me remind you once more that the Catholic teaching about capital, or private and productive ownership, is the *via media* between the two contradictory theories to which is to be traced the present strained relations obtaining between Capital and Labour.

The Catholic Church on the one hand rigidly insists that it is a sin against nature to proclaim that man is the absolute proprietor of all that he possesses, and that he may convert it to any use he may think fit, regardless of the needs of his fellow-man. On the other hand, the Catholic Church no less insists that it is a sin against nature to proclaim that all property is robbery, and that under the plea of philanthropy or what not, it ought to be transferred to the community and socialized.

The Catholic Church condemns and has always condemned, as the writings of St. Thomas of

Aquin, who wrote on the subject luminously six hundred years ago, abundantly testifies, both these contradictory theories about ownership. The Church takes her stand between these two conflicting dogmas about private property. Recognizing that man in order to realize himself and to fulfil his mission in life as an individual and as head of a family, must possess some sort of property, she says that God, who is the One, supreme Proprietor of the Goods of the earth, has given over to man the control and management of property, but only as His stewards; so that while he may make use of so much of it as is necessary for the support and up-keep of his station in life, he is bound under pain of sin to distribute of his superfluities to those of his brethren who stand in need of them. The Catholic Church upholds and safeguards the right of private and productive ownership in the sense I have explained.

But while she thus sets her face as flint against the iniquitous doctrine that property is robbery, she utters her anathemas no less clearly and distinctly against the dictum that a man may do just as he pleases with what is called his own.

Let me repeat, man is God's steward and will have to give an account of his stewardship. He will have to give an account of how he got his property, of how he managed his property, and of how he used his property, and also of how he resisted the encroachments of those who dared to lay hands on his property, forgetting or ignoring the divine precepts: "Thou shalt not steal," "Thou shalt not covet thy neighbour's goods."

Defend your private property. Remember that it represents the labours of your father, the solicitudes of your mother; remember that in defending it you are guarding your home, you are protecting your children, you are providing for your family, you are upholding those two strong pillars — Property and Family — on which your country depends for its material and natural support, strength, and stability.

IX

SOCIALISM AND ITS PROMISES

IT is only by going among the people and inter-changing talk with them that you can arrive at a true and just estimate of what they are, of what they have, and of what they really think about such problems as Socialism and kindred subjects. When you win the confidence of the workingman he keeps nothing back; he utters his soul, he re-veals his inner self, and gladly puts before you his aims and ambitions in life.

During my travels from the Hudson to the Yukon, and whilst steaming on the Pacific Ocean and its big tributary rivers, I made a point of associating, when opportunity offered, with the various sections of the toiling classes who were my fellow-travellers. Invariably, after a very short interval, they made me feel quite at home with them, making me the companion of their thoughts and extending to me the hand of welcome and of friendship.

You will ask me: "Did you find them innocu-lated with the microbe of Socialism? Were they among those who believe in the 'redemption of the people by the people'?" I must confess that quite a considerable section of them showed very decided leanings towards Socialism. On one occasion, whilst chatting with a group of men, made up of several nationalities, and following various callings, from that of the mechanician to the logger, our conversation drifted to Socialism, and all its fair promises. The chief spokesman of the party, a broad-shouldered, rough-spun looking overseer of a railway gang of metal layers, said his reading had made it clear to him that it was the Catholic Church which had created capitalism and the various constitutions making up the different governments ruling the world to-day. He said that no other Church counted for much among the working classes, and he contended that the Catholic Church itself was losing ground every day; that Socialism was drawing thence some of its best recruits. It was his strong conviction that once Catholics got fused into true Socialism, they had no more use for the Church than "a chauffeur for a push cart." I asked him what in his opinion was it that drew the Catholic toiler into the socialist net? He replied at once: "First of all, Catholics who want to get on in any kind of business begin by joining what you call the Secret Societies, and once they have got in there they shed their religion as surely as the deer its horns. Besides," he continued, "all religions are the out-put of economic conditions, and though your Church in a day gone by may have done something for the workingman, her day is passed; she is as much behind the times as the drill and hammer are behind the dredger. She is a low-grade proposition, and will never again strike gold." I reminded my friend of what the Catholic Church was doing to-day in the United States, and with some pride I drew out not a short list of her great and glorious achievements. But he only shrugged his shoulders, and said, "Maybe she is all you say, but she is losing her hold for all that, and her loss is our gain. We are netting them like Alaskan salmon, and no mistake about it."

With rare exceptions the bread-winner outside the Church seems to be pretty fully convinced that the coming religion, so-called, of the workingman is going to be "Class Religion"; that is to say, a "religion" making directly for the material and social interests of the toiling classes, and indirectly for the social well-being of humanity.

Socialists are very plausible and most insinuating. They have a patent medicine which is a cure-all for every conceivable grievance and complaint. The vote-catching Socialist will tell his hearers that it is the high mission of Socialism to relieve all the woes and wrongs from which the social organism is at present suffering; that when once the Commonwealth shall have been established in their midst, there will no longer be any occasion for penury or want, and that all social and class distinctions will then be done away with forever, while in the place of capital and labour, of peer and peasant, of rich and poor, there will rise up a common Brotherhood with money enough and leisure enough to go right round. Then life will become worth living, for no man will be overworked or underpaid, while members of the community will be assured of all that is needed to make their lot in life one of contentment and of merriment; in a word, one of earthly happiness.

When the socialist agitator finds himself in an agricultural district, with an audience made up of labourers and small farmers, he unfolds another tale. He expatiates upon the wrongs done to the small landholder by the millionnaire farmer with his countless acres under wheat or other cereals, and with outstanding lands laden with lumber. "These are the thieves," he will tell his gaping auditory, "who are robbing you of a decent price for your crops, these are the landowners who are underselling you ; see, here are the grafters who are manipulating the railroads, and making it impossible for you to pay the freight of your produce to the nearest city market. You have a real grievance, you have," exclaims the agitator. "For you there is no redress but Socialism. Under our Commonwealth you will be the men to benefit most of all, for you will become in the socialist State the chief producers of grain and other food-stuffs. No longer will you be beaten to the earth by the savage competition set up by landlord capitalists ; we shall see that you will have fair play, fair pay, and a market, which shall under no conditions be cornered by a group of men, or by any single individual. If you want to stick to the land, if you want to have fine crops with an assured market, throw in your lot with us, who are your friends, who wish you well, and who will make life for the small holder worth while. Lift up your voices, and let your cry loud and strong be: 'On to Socialism.'"

On the other hand, when the socialist orator's platform is not in the country, but in a busy city his cry is changed to "Down with the Department Store." He gathers round his soap box the small storekeepers with their customers and discourses to them eloquently about the iniquities of "the Universal Provider." "But for these big ventures, but for these colossal stores, you," he shouts out, "would be doing in this town a thriving business. It is the millionnaire store which you are up against, which is starving you, and which is ruining and closing up all the retail businesses in this city." Then the socialist agitator will go on to assure his storekeeping friends that he and his fellows have made it their mission to study the present iniquitous condition of affairs which has rendered it impossible for an honest tradesman to hold his own, and to keep his door open to the public. "When once we have made a clean sweep of these sky-scraping department premises, you," he goes on to say, "will have it all your own way, you will make a fine turnover, for we shall see that instead of having to compete in a heavily handicapped race for the necessaries of life, you will, on the contrary, be assured a comfortable income on which to live and enjoy the good things of time and sense. If you want to thrive instead of starve, if you want success instead of bankruptcy, come over to our camp. Unite with us, and we will make short shift of these inhuman business competitors. In their place and on their premises, we will set up your stores, and from you only shall be purchased all hardware goods, fancy articles, clothing, groceries, drugs, farming implements, household utensils, and other salable articles recognized by our Commonwealth. Rally to our red flag, for under it, and under it only, will you find your businesses supreme, and your income assured, and your own lives for the first time without an anxiety, a debt, or a trouble. Your hours of work will be few and your time of leisure ample."

There is yet another section of the community to which the socialist campaigner never forgets to make an appeal as telling as it is specious. It is to the agnostic, to the unbeliever, and to the atheist that he pours forth from street corners and meeting rooms a very torrent of his choicest eloquence. Mounting his rostrum, he reminds the groups of non-religious or irreligious men met about him, that in a free country a man should be entitled to hold what views he likes about the religious question; that whereas under the present régime men who are without some label or other of superstitious belief are looked down upon by a cant-loving community with suspicion, and are treated as though they were some pestilence-breeding swamp to be shunned and condemned as unclean and unfit for citizenship, under

Socialism, on the contrary, it will be the men not hampered and tethered and narrowed by religious sentiments, and the worn-out beliefs of a bygone dark age, who will find the most hearty welcome from the comrades. "No longer will you find yourselves blackballed because you happen to have the courage of your convictions." "Religion," the special pleading socialist rhetorician goes on to assure his audience, "is no concern of ours; it is a private affair; do as you will about it; only come and rally to our platform. Lift up your eloquence, pour forth your views, lend us your noble spirit of independence with which to advocate our cause which is identified with your own. We need the support of men like you, who are not priest-ridden. Turn to us and in turn we will do you honour, we will give you our confidence, and will in a day, not far hence, raise you to positions of trust and distinction. Give us your two hands and let us unite, for we have interests in common, and both of us believe in shaking off all tyrannical forms of religion, as well as the iniquitous competition of all capital." In a Western city of America I stood on the fringe of a well-dressed crowd cheering to the echo an orator whose peroration to his anti-religious harangue was a prayer addressed to a dollar which he had drawn forth from his vest pocket, and which he told his hearers, with their almost unanimous approval, was the only god who nowadays heard the workingman's prayer, gave him food, and drink, home and clothing, and a good time generally. Before he had ended I slipped away to the nearest police officer, and asked him if he could direct me to some recognized socialist meeting. He pointed to the crowd from which I had come. "That," I said, "is not a gathering of Socialists but of atheists, I have this moment left them." "It is all the same," replied the officer; "when once they let themselves go, I guess they always carry on like that."

There are occasions when the socialist agitator does not let himself go, but is more guarded in his speech. When he happens to be in some more Catholic district, and is angling for the Catholic vote, the Socialist can assume an air almost of piety. I well remember on a dusky Sunday evening, in the fall of 1911, being drawn to a gathering in an Eastern city park. High above the closely packed meeting stood a well-dressed, well-set-up socialist agitator who was carefully surveying and manipulating his audience. After instructing them about his own merits, and informing them that though personally he belonged to no church, yet he contended there was room in Socialism for church-going people. He went on to say that Socialists might believe as much as they cared to swallow of what priests and parsons chose to toss out to them. " Clergymen have a right," he said, "to express their own individual views about religion in the way they happen to think best. We do not want to hold you back from accepting what they can no more prove than you yourselves can. My friends, follow, if you will, their creed, but shun their politics. Do not believe a word they say about Socialism, which is purely a political question, a question as much outside religion as the Post-office or any other economic problem. Catholics," he continued, "are beginning in this liberty-loving land to wake up; they are thinking for themselves, and are finding out that the priesthood is stepping on dangerous ground when it dictates to the American Irish and Germans what they are to think of the socialist Commonwealth." He turned to his hearers and had the assurance to tell them that the sons of Erin and of the Fatherland were being recruited into the ranks of Socialism by the thousand. He concluded his impassioned address by urging his hearers not to take their

Y

politics from Rome, or from any one commissioned
by Rome, but to look round for themselves and
to sever once and for all their political from their
religious creed, and to unite with Socialists in
breaking down all class distinction, and all capitalist exploitation of labour.   This astute speaker
made a point of praising and thanking the Irish
and Germans in America for their sympathy and
support, and concluded his address by insinuating
that under a socialist régime it would fall more
especially to the Celtic race to become their
leaders, who, by their native eloquence and skill,
were best fitted to shape and direct the socialist
State to its most glorious destiny — the realization of human happiness on earth.

From what I have said you will allow that the
Socialist is, as I heard an Indian half-breed in
Montana observe, not a bad angler; one who
knows how "to bait his hook, and meat his trap
for eats."   On a wheel-stern, flat-bottomed boat
I was steaming up the Yukon.   Suddenly we
drew alongside a lumber yard to wood up and
feed our engines.   One of the crew with whom I
happened to be in conversation hurried away,
trundling his wheelbarrow.   As he did so he
observed : "You see, Father, we can't carry
enough wood to make the round.   Between Daw-

son and White Horse we have to log up six times. I guess the socialist Ship of State, of which we have been speaking, will not be able to carry enough stuff to go round, neither." That is just it. Even on the supposition that we did socialize all the instruments of production and distribution of wealth, there would not be enough to go round. We should be brought to a dead standstill. Individuals might get their "labour ticket," but would they find what they wanted? All commodities would be on an official pattern, and you would be compelled on all occasions to conform your wants and tastes to "our own make," with the unlovely consequence that life would be as deadly dull as that seen in a boarding-house, a charity school, or a barrack room. You would never be able to exchange the "State label" for any special or select brand more to your liking. I rather fancy the government-labelled article would itself run short.

But this would be but one of many difficulties. How about the organization of the socialist State? In the United States, with its 80,000,000 of population, and its many diverse interests, and its varied climate, and its peoples made up of every nation under the sun, would it be at all possible, even to dream in one's wildest dreams, of any

practical scheme by which such an ever expand-
ing and ever shifting population could be welded
by some central power, with its agents all over
the States, into an harmoniously working Commonwealth? Why, the idea even of such a possibility is an insanity; it argues a plentiful lack
of knowledge of the peoples making up this vast
community, and it betrays a pitiful ignorance of
the condition of things necessarily prevailing in
a young, vigorous, enterprising, and venture-
loving population. A socialist Commonwealth
in any single city in the States, say, in New York,
or Chicago, or San Francisco, or Boston, would
not last till the close of the day on which it was
set up. In spite of the special pleading of Messrs.
Bellamy, Hillquit, Spargo, and other optimists,
it would be altogether beyond the powers of
any socialist Commonwealth to satisfy American
citizens that they had been assigned their right
place and their right task in the new Republic.
The shoe-shiner, for instance, might think he
ought to be the druggist, the schoolmaster might
want to be the physician, the motorman might
wonder why he was not the dentist, and most
probably no one in the community at all would
allow that he ought to be the city scavenger,
the sewer-man, coal-heaver, night-watchman,

or the asylum or prison warden. How, let me ask, is Socialism going to organize labour in a measure to satisfy even the most pious of its comrades? Not long ago I happened to hear a guest in a hotel call a waiter to order for neglect of duty. The ready answer tossed back to him was this: "Before long you will have to wait on yourself, and unless you get black or yellow help, I guess you will also have to cook for yourself; we are nearly through with all these class differences." I asked my table waiter whether that man had expressed the view prevailing generally among waiters. "Yes," he replied, "we are most of us comrades now, and we do not believe that we are going to wait much longer on those at whose table we shall not have a right to eat." He added, "My sister is a lady-help out West, but I guess she eats with the family."

Here, for the moment, let us suppose that all the means of production and distribution of wealth have been duly socialized, that the organization of work has successfully been put into operation, and that every comrade in the newly established Commonwealth is fully satisfied with the part assigned him to play in it. So far, well; but here comes in another big and difficult problem, the question of remuneration. Would it be possible so to draw up a sliding scale of prices for services that every comrade would be contented with what fell to his lot? I have a shrewd suspicion that human nature, being as it is at present found among the socialist body, it would be no easy task to draft a scheme, or draw out a schedule, that would be approved and indorsed by the workers. Under a socialist régime no one would think that he had enough if somebody else had more. Why should he? On socialist showing one man is as good as another; his only claim to a higher remuneration than another being his greater usefulness to the community. On this principle, the sewage of a city being of more vital importance than its artistic proportions, the street sweeper would receive a better "labour ticket" than the city architect. Perhaps the architect himself might feel aggrieved, but there would be no redress. The question of remuneration in a socialist State has never been fairly met and solved for the very simple reason that it does not admit of solution. You can no more solve it than you can solve the question of motive. There is no incentive to work but motive. Without some adequative motive, human or divine, to impel a man to work, you will not get anything worth having out of him. He will be without heart, without pride in the work set him, because while you may have given him a task to fulfil, you have robbed him of the motive power with which to accomplish it. Man not being an automatic machine, but a human being, to get top speed and good service out of him you must do more than crank up and provide gasolene; you must supply motive. Man's character needs grading up to lofty and holy principles if he is to accomplish great things for creed and country. Indeed, it is no exaggeration to say that in the measure in which a man is actuated by motives noble, lofty, and chivalrous will his life become a worthy inspiration to others.

We are assured by modern Socialists that the manufacturer, banker, and tradesman may be stimulated by the hope of financial success in business, but not so the scientist. All that he cares for is "the recognition accorded to him by the learned fraternity." Give him academic distinctions and he will be happy. On the other hand, the artist, Messrs. Hillquit, Spargo, and other leading lights of the Socialist party tell us, seeks neither the reward of money nor of academic titles. He sets no value on anything but "public applause and glory." So, too, the statesman and the soldier. Both of these public servants are actu-

ated by a longing for "authority and influence."
Money, honours, and glory to them are of no
value whatever.

What a pitiful ignorance of human nature
does not all this balderdash betray! Do artists,
then, give their paintings away for a mere song,
or knock them down to the highest bidder at an
auction sale? Perhaps there is no class of men
with a more passionate love of beautiful and
rare things than the artistic class. The man with
an artistic temperament needs money to purchase
these treasures. He wants examples. He needs
models. He must study the masterpieces in
gallery, cathedral, and museum. To confine
the artist to a socialist State would be like yok-
ing a thoroughbred to a plough, like chaining a
husky to a kennel, like confining an eagle to a
cage.

Socialists when pleading for their Commonwealth must not forget that men are not to be
driven, and that they are not to be converted by
acts of a socialist State, nor sanctified by processes
of logic.

Under a socialist State the special pleading
Socialist thinks that there would be no difficulty
in engaging your hewer of wood, drawer of water,
your drain-worker, and your scullery maid. They

are difficult enough to get now, and you may be sure that under a socialist State they would not be get-at-able at all. For then the guarantee would have to be : "The maximum of freedom and of pay with the minimum of work and restraint !"

X

SOCIALISM AND SOCIAL REFORMATION

SOCIALISTS have laid us under a deep indebtedness in two ways. In the first place, they have set us a splendid example not only of energy and of enterprise in working for a cause, but they have also shown us a spirit of generosity, not to say of self-sacrifice, by the way they go to work in their attempt to establish a Commonwealth with a very problematical future and a very uncertain destiny. In the second place they have done a great and valuable work in calling our attention to the social evils of the day. In fact, reading the history of Socialism is almost like reading the history of the quest for the philosopher's stone which was to transmute all metals into gold. The object sought for in both cases is unattainable. You can no more revolutionize human nature than you can turn iron into gold. Yet the search in both cases has resulted in a number of by-products not without their use. Alchemy gave an impetus to modern chemistry, and has not Socialism given incentive to social science, to which many Socialists have contributed valuable service?

Indeed, if all socialist literature had reached the level, say, of such books as "Industrial Democracy," we could regard Socialism with different eyes from which actually we do. Alas, a glance at my book shelves reminds me that the gospel of Socialism has, in the main, been a gospel of hatred, of fanaticism, and of class division.

Yet, once again, let me say it, Socialists have done good service in revealing our social wrongs and injustices, in denouncing our avarice and cruelty, and in showing up our crass stupidity and smug pharisaism. True, they are not alone in their denunciation; I might cite a long list of earnest men of all shades of religious and political creeds who have done the same.

Righteous indignation at injustice, and strenuous endeavour to right it, spring spontaneous from human nature wherever it is found unspoiled, and I am one who firmly believes that the spirit to make what is all wrong all right is a spirit that is growing all the time.

It is with deep reluctance that on such a day as this, which the Lord hath made, that I pass into questions of controversy.[1] With still greater reluctance do I utter a word of condemnation of a party made up of men and women who, let us try to believe, are struggling for a larger measure of justice to their fellows. But after paying my debt of praise to Socialists for having arrested and fixed the attention of lawmakers, capitalists, philanthropists, and others on the many social sores and industrial burdens weighing down and hurting the workingman, I must part company with them; I cannot call them "comrades."

As a man and a Christian I am compelled to condemn Socialism first, because, whether I consider it from the standpoint of history or from the outlook of Christian ethics, I find it to be bound up with principles and postulates and consequences which by no legitimate mental process can be made to fit in with the laws of justice, equity, and right as promulgated by the Christian Dispensation.

Secondly, as a man and a Christian I condemn Socialism because, even if it were an economic theory only, which it is not, it would still be

[1] This Conference was delivered on Easter Sunday, before 7000 persons, who were packed to the limits of standing room. It was estimated by the press that as many were turned away an hour before service.

fraught, as I have pointed out in my previous Conferences, with consequences pernicious and even disastrous to the individual and to the family, to religion and to the State.

Thirdly, I condemn Socialism because it takes for granted what is not true, that all the social and industrial evils of our day are wrongs inherent in the system of private capital.

It will not do vividly to portray the troubles and the wrongs of the wage-earning classes — their cold and hunger, their poverty or penury, their want of wage and of work, their wretchedness and misery, and, then, with a lightning jump of logic, to exclaim: "This is all due to and is a necessary consequence of the private ownership of the means of production." We must proceed calmly and surely in judgment, and before passing a verdict on a case involving such tremendous issues, as does the one before us, we must first of all give a patient hearing to both sides of the case, bearing in mind that, while on the one hand Socialists saddle upon capital the entire responsibility and burden of all our present-day social wrongs, there are on the other hand thousands of their fellow-citizens, men upright of purpose, sound in judgment, students of history, well read in sociology; ripe scholars and earnest

Christians solicitous, nay, most anxious, to safeguard the rights of all their fellow-countrymen, who declare that the social evils, of which both parties alike complain, are not due to nor essentially inherent in private ownership, but, on the contrary, are due almost entirely to certain economic and industrial abuses that have been imported into the system. Nay, I will go further and will say with Leo XIII, and the Supreme Pontiff now sitting on the Throne of the Fisherman, that if only the principles of Christian justice and Christian charity as taught in the Christianity of Christ had been observed and enforced in the relations between capital and labor, the said abuses never could have arisen, never could have crept into the system hitherto obtaining. Be sure of this, that our present-day struggles, our present-day evils, and our present-day situation of unrest and of rivalry, of class hatred, and of fight for bigger dividends and higher wages, are in no small measure the outcome of apostacy from God, and revolt against Christ and His Christianity.

If this world is our be-all and our end-all, then, let the cure-all for the present chaotic condition to which, through our own folly, we have brought ourselves, be revolution, with a policy of universal grab. The alternative before us is what I have stated once and again in the course of these Conferences, either on to Socialism or back to Christ.

It is possible that some of my hearers may still retain something of complacency and satisfaction with a condition of things which has provoked the denunciations of many true social reformers. For I fear that the social sense of many of us is still in a very rudimentary condition. Some I fear have hardened their hearts by self-indulgence and luxury. Others are merely stupid and lacking in imagination. They do not know what the hungry and homeless feel like, therefore hunger and homelessness do not exist. Their complacency is increased by a certain type of anti-socialist literature, which to my mind is as harmful as the literature which it seeks to combat. If anything could make me a Socialist it would be the anti-socialist literature which is controlled by men who are growing rich on unjust profits, and is devoted to misrepresenting the condition of the working classes and distorting or entirely ignoring their grievances. Such literature is wholly opposed to the spirit of Christianity. It is an attempt to stifle the voice of the oppressed, which cries to Heaven for vengeance.

Some of our social evils spring from deliberate injustice. Others spring from stupidity. Together they amount to an appalling sum of misery which must be faced honestly and remedied promptly. Lest any of my readers should think I am exaggerating, let me recall a few facts about social conditions in my own country. I leave it to you to say if things are better here in your own land. I take from the English Catholic Social Year Book for 1910: —

1. The Housing of the Poor is a national disgrace. This evil is largely responsible for much of our physical and moral degradation. Seven hundred thousand dwellings in England are said to be insanitary or overcrowded. Two and a half millions of people are declared to be living in overcrowded tenements. "Millions of human beings are housed worse than the cattle or horses of many a lord or squire. . . . What delicacy, modesty, or self-respect can be expected of men and women whose bodies are so shamefully packed together?"

2. One out of every four persons in London dies in a workhouse, asylum, or hospital, and over 30 per cent of the population of London live on or below the poverty line. Unemployment in threatening proportions is ever with us.

3. Infant mortality due to criminal carelessness or curable ignorance is deplorably high. The

figures are sufficiently startling, but they by no means represent the reality. Sir John Gorst writes: —

"I am assured by doctors who are in actual practice in our cities that such figures give no idea of the infant mortality among the poor, and that they know of streets where more than half the children born alive perish under a year old."

4. Of intemperance in England, Cardinal Manning wrote: —

"It is no rhetoric nor exaggeration nor fanaticism to affirm that intemperance in intoxicating drink is a vice that stands head and shoulders above all the vices by which we are afflicted; and that . . . we are preëminent in this scandal and shame; and that intemperance in intoxicating drink may, in sad and sober truth, be called our national vice."

5. Wages are frequently far below that minimum upon which the Catholic Church insists as necessary for decent living.

In spite of recent improvements, sweating still persists to an appalling extent in the old countries, not only 'in the case of home workers, but also in many factories and workshops. With the sweating evil goes child labor, and a Medical Superintendent Officer of Health tells us that: —

z

"In the poorest and most unhealthy of our dwellings this variety of home work is carried on to an inconceivable extent, and in some streets one could hardly enter a house without seeing two, three, four or more children, varying in age from six to twelve years, sitting round a table, all intensely busy trying to earn a miserable pittance."

Let me give an example from an American writer. He was in a glass factory where he noticed that the "carrying-in boys" had been replaced by automatic machinery. The reason of this, said the manager of the factory, was due to the fact they could not get the boys they needed. In another factory boys were still "carrying-in," and the reason of it there was that they could not manage to get on without them. When reminded that automatic machinery could accomplish what was being done by boys, there came the ready reply: "Why should I tie up two or three thousand dollars of my capital to install machinery? So long as I can get any supply of lads I don't want to bother about machinery."

Clearly the only way of stopping the employment of boys, at enormous cost of life, in unhealthy factories, is legislation. We must not wait till Capital takes pity on Labor.

"In the United Kingdom," we are told that "out of a population of 43,000,000, as many as 38,000,000 are poor. . . . The United Kingdom is seen to contain a great multitude of poor people veneered with a thin layer of the comfortable and the rich. . . . In an average year eight millionnaires die, leaving between them three times as much wealth as is left by 644,000 poor persons who die in one year. Again, in a single average year, the wealth left by the few rich people who die approaches in amount the aggregate property possessed by the whole of the living poor. . . . About one-seventieth part of the population owns far more than one-half of the entire accumulated wealth, public and private, of the United Kingdom." (Chizza, " Money, Poverty, and Riches," pp. 43, 52, 72.) Mr. Hunter, referring to this same subject, tells us in his work on "Poverty" (p. 60) that ten millions of the people of the United States are sunk in poverty, while four millions of them are in receipt of relief.

In 1854 there were not more than twenty-five millionnaires in New York City, their total fortunes aggregating $43,000,000. There were not more than fifty millionnaires in the whole of the United States, their aggregate fortunes not exceeding $80,000,000. To-day there are several individual fortunes of more than $80,000,000 each. New York City alone is said to have over two thousand millionnaires, and the United States more than five thousand. The writer goes on to observe that : "it is only necessary to add that all the millionnaires of 1854, together with the half millionnaires, owned not more than about $100,000,000 out of the total wealth, which was at that time something like $10,000,000,000. In other words, they owned not more than one per cent of the wealth of the country. In 1890, when the wealth of the country was slightly more than $65,000,000,000, Senator Ingalls could quote in the United States Senate a table showing that the millionnaires and half millionnaires of that time, 31,100 persons in all, owned $36,250,000,000, or just fifty-six per cent of the entire wealth of the United States."

A modern writer reminds us that "the figures furnished by the United States Bureau of Labor indicate that the wage in American cities is not sufficient to enable a man with a wife and family of three children under fourteen years of age to maintain a decent standard of living. In the larger cities $3 a day, and in the smaller, less expensive cities $2.50, are the least wages upon which a standard of decency can be maintained."

"Corroborative evidence of these statements may readily be secured in any locality by personal observation which will convince even the most sceptical that the standard of American wages for semiskilled and unskilled labor is considerably below $2 a day."

The immigrants accept the low wages and live on low standards without realizing the results of their action. They think in terms of Europe and accept employment at a wage far below that necessary for the maintenance of family efficiency, or even of family life in the United States. They are unacquainted with prices and the cost of living, and their judgment is therefore dependent not upon knowledge of American conditions, but upon that of foreign conditions. "The newcomers know nothing of a standard wage, and when work is scarce, they will offer to work for less than is paid common labor. Such was the case of a band of Croatians who offered their services to a firm in Pittsburg for $1.20 a day. When the superintendent heard it, he said, 'My God, what is the country coming to! How can a man live in Pittsburg on $1.20 a day?' The foreman replied, 'Give them rye bread, a herring, and beer, and they are all right.'"

The immigrants thus establish a "single man"

foreign standard for American wages, and fore-
men and superintendents, by using the foreigners,
succeed in reducing the wages of the American
workmen. "Shrewd superintendents are known,
not only to take advantage of the influx of unskilled labor to keep down day wages, but to reduce the pay of skilled men by a gradually enforced
system of promoting the Slavs." [1] I am told that
95.4 per cent of the tailors on the Island of Man-
hattan, N.Y., are or were foreigners, and in Chicago,
81.8 per cent are so.

" The silk mills in some parts of the anthracite
region of Pennsylvania work night and day. It
is much cheaper. As a manufacturer said, 'You
get your money for 3 per cent.' Across the
street from one of these mills stands a wooden
miner's shanty. One night an old man and a
little boy walked out on the porch of this home,
and the old man leaned down and kissed the boy's
forehead. 'Good night, father,' said the boy,
and taking his dinner pail from where it stood
on the porch, he walked slowly across the street,
and into the lighted mill for the night shift.
Twelve hours later he stumbled sleepily across
the same street, into the miner's shanty, and went

[1] "The New Pittsburgers," Peter Roberts, *Charities and the
Commons*, Jan. 2, 1909, Vol. 21, p. 538.

to bed. He had done his 'turn' on the night shift, away from home, all night long in the mill, with some rough women and some rougher men; then during the day he must sleep while he can, preparatory to another twelve hours in the mill. Children who work 'night shift' do not participate in the duties and pleasures of home life. Child labour eliminates the child labourer from the life of the home, and therefore becomes a problem of the family as well as a problem of the child."

With instances such as these before us we may readily understand how the toiling classes snatch, like the drowning man, at any plank thrown out to them by the paid agitator; live they cannot without a living wage. At best there is before the toiler but a short existence. Mr. Scott Nealing assures us that: "The length of life is determined, not by any inherent incapacity in man to live, but by the maladjustment surrounding the living and working conditions.

"There is also a considerable variation of the length of life within the same country.[1] Men born in American cities of native white parents live on the average only 31 years; those born of foreign white parents live 29.1 years; while those

[1] "Modern Social Conditions," W. B. Bailey, New York, The Century Co., 1906, p. 227.

born of colored parents live only 26.3 years. These figures will prove a rude shock to the contented citizens who were congratulating themselves upon the supposition that men lived threescore and ten years or thereabouts. Men do not live even half of threescore and ten years in the modern American city, but die, on the average, when they reach the age of one score and ten.

"Variation in the length of life thus occurs with locality, race, and sex, but from the standpoint of the present study no variation is of such profound significance as the variation between occupations.

"Many men die because of the occupation in which they are engaged. There is a very direct connection between mortality and occupation."[1]

Consider for a moment the lives of those who in England card hooks and eyes for one penny a gross, who make our match-boxes (288 drawers, 288 covers, 288 bits of sandpaper) for twopence half penny per gross, who birl and kink fringes on shawls for less than a penny per hour, who convert sugar bags into bran sacks for one penny per dozen, who make artificial flowers for threepence or fourpence the gross. Excluding domestic servants, there are in England $3\frac{1}{2}$ million wage-earning women, and

[1] Social Adjustment.

thousands of them receiving less than 7 shillings a week. Only to think of it — in London, where there is no room but in its churches, one fifth of the population underfed and overcrowded!

The list might be prolonged, but enough has, perhaps, been said to prove the indictment against us.

Clearly, therefore, as Pope Leo told us, "a remedy must be found and found speedily" for such a condition of affairs. What is the remedy to be? I repeat, not Socialism. For Socialism, as I have endeavoured to show, would cripple the forces which are indispensable for social welfare.

Not legislation alone. Legislation can but indirectly touch the deeper springs of national wellbeing. How can it foster kindly relations between employer and employed, or strengthen conjugal fidelity, or kindle patriotism or inculcate generosity, manliness, thrift? It may help to remove obstacles to the development of these qualities, but it can scarcely do more.

Moreover, legislation, unless supported by public opinion, is almost useless. You may pass your laws, but they will be evaded unless a healthy social conscience among the people insures their application. How much social legislation in the past has become a dead letter owing to the fact that the public, which may have pressed for a measure of reform, is apt to lose interest in it as soon as it is secured.

What we want on both sides of the Atlantic is a highly developed social conscience — a trained alertness on the part of all citizens to use every fraction of their social influence in getting, first of all, present laws enforced. We need a considerable development of private initiative all over the country. But again, no form of private initiative will suffice by itself to solve the social question. Private initiative cannot control the required resources; and in the last resort it cannot exercise the needed compulsion. A thousand men unite in beneficent private enterprise: ten men stand out. Those ten may foil the efforts of the thousand. The selfish individualism of the few may actually make iniquitous profit from the efforts of the many. "In the kingdom of private social enterprise the rascal is king," to adapt an old proverb. The strong arm of the law must be brought in to dislodge him from his fastness. As Pope Leo says, "If employers lay unjust burdens upon their workmen or degrade them with conditions repugnant to their dignity as human beings it is right to invoke the assistance and authority of the law."

Nor can the Christianity of Christ alone solve the social question. For the social question is not merely a moral or religious question. It is an economic and political question as well. It demands the positive action of civil authority. This point is insisted on by Leo XIII. I wish to lay stress on it here because I am presently going to insist upon the fact that the social question cannot be solved apart from Christian principles, and that the Church must have a large share in its solution. Some ardent Christians have jumped to the conclusion that it is the task of the Church to solve the social question unaided, and that the office of the civil authority consists merely in protecting mens' rights. This is not the case. State action, and private action, too, must combine with Church action in the solution of the social question. That is the common view of Catholics based on the teaching of Leo XIII. It would seem to be the only reasonable view.

There can be no short cut, no simple remedy, no panacea. All possible forces must be brought to bear on the question; and they must be co-ordinated. Legislation and private endeavour and Christian enterprise must unite and combine, each supporting the other.

Let us take these three instruments of social

regeneration one by one, and see what each is actually doing, and how each might be further strengthened. Finally, we may consider how their action may be correlated and used to the best advantage so as to secure some reasonable solution of this terrible and terrifying problem.

1. Legislation.

Considerable progress has been made in social legislation during the past century. With the reaction against the old *laissez faire* principle came one measure after another destined to secure for the worker decent conditions of life and labour.

I need not repeat the story of the passing of Factory laws in Europe and America. Sanitation and safety have to a large measure been secured to our workers; children have been rescued in many places from the worst horrors of factory slavery; the hours of labour have been regulated at least to some extent. Contrast the conditions of labour now with those in the early part of the nineteenth century and it will be seen that enormous progress has been made.

Glance for a moment at the list of laws that have been passed since England woke up to find herself a Democracy! The Workmens' Compensation Act, an Old Age Pension Act, The Trades

Disputes Act. I might lengthen out this catalogue of laws for the betterment of our people, but I will content myself with the mention of a few more measures which go to show how rapidly the Old Country has rattled along the road called Social Reform during the past decade. There is the Small Holdings Act, The House and Town-planning Act. Then there is The Childrens' Charter, and The Insurance Scheme, and a score of other measures, which time will reveal, for the uplifting, the betterment, and the comfort and happiness of the toilers in this great Workshop called the world.

From England the principle of factory legislation spread to the United States, Germany, France, and Switzerland, and finally it established itself in all industrial countries.

"Looking broadly now to labour legislation as it has occurred in this country," says Mr. Carroll D. Wright, speaking of factory laws in the United States, "it may be well to sum up its general features. Such legislation has fixed the hours of labour for women and certain minors in manufacturing establishments; it has adjusted the contracts of labour; it has protected employees by insisting that all dangerous machinery shall be guarded; . . . it has created boards of factory inspectors, whose powers and duties have added much to the health and safety of the operatives; it has in many instances provided for weekly payments, not only by municipalities, but by corporations; . . . it has regulated the employment of prisoners; protected the employment of children; exempted the wages of the wife and minor children from attachment; established bureaus for statistics of labour; provided for the ventilation of factories and workshops; established industrial schools and evening schools; provided special transportation by railroads for workingmen; modified the common-law rules relative to the liability of employers for injuries of their employees; fixed the compensation of railroad corporations for negligently causing the death of employees, and has provided for their protection against accident and death."

After all this progress, however, we are still only in the beginning of our democratic campaign of life-saving. To conserve life and health, society must enormously increase its efforts along present lines and must open up new routes of progress.

Perhaps there is no question demanding closer or more immediate study than the question of wages. And on this point I must say a word.

The "just wage" is a matter upon which the Catholic Church holds very strong views. She detests the old political economy which concentrated its attention merely on production. She looks to the producer. The workman has a right to a living wage, and legislation should enforce that right.

In England the demand by miners for a living minimum wage commands our sympathy, because the wage in many instances is low, taking into consideration the hardness of the work and its risks to life and limb. Besides, we must not forget that the profits from some of the British mines have been quite enormous. But it is a little difficult to see the justice of a demand for a minimum wage which every worker should receive, altogether irrespective of his efficiency and of the amount of work that he does. In one of the New York dailies I found the matter well put. Speaking on this question the writer says:—

"If that should be granted in the mines the same demand might be extended into other industries and occupations, in some of which, indeed, conditions call for it at least as much as in the collieries. There would be established the principle for which many Socialists have contended, that every man, whether competent or incompetent, whether industrious or lazy, shall receive from somebody a sum sufficient for his needs." Now, it is true that every man ought to get a living income, but it is equally true that every able-bodied man ought to earn his wages.

"It is true also that with the minimum wage established there would be a possibility of paying higher wages to the more efficient men, though more than one big strike has arisen from the objection of labour unions to that very thing. The point is, however, that there would be nothing to prevent a lazy workman from 'soldiering' and producing only a fraction of what he could and should produce, feeling secure in the receipt of the minimum wage and in the assurance that his union on pain of striking would not permit his employer to dismiss him for inefficiency. The minimum wage would be all right if it were earned and if there were an assurance that it would be earned, or at least that workmen would faithfully do their work. To say that every man shall receive at least so much and that there shall be no dismissals for incompetency would be to offer a temptation to idleness.

"*The Westminster Gazette*, which strongly supports the present government and which takes the radical side in such disputes as this, puts the matter well when it says that 'the right plan is to give the men collectively an incentive to keep up the output and to deal themselves with the lazy or inefficient worker whose malingering would reduce it.' That is indisputable; but the question is how the men are to be induced, under the minimum wage system, to establish and maintain such a standard. And that is a problem which may confront America as well as England."

It is not my business to draw up a scheme of social legislation. I merely wish to point out that much remains to be studied. Let me further insist on the need of rescuing such legislation from its subordination to mere party interests. Valuable as the party system may be, it should not be allowed to prejudice the progress of beneficial legislation. We need a great diffusion of social conscience in the community which will elevate the vital interests of the nation above the strife of parties, and secure a consistent and well-calculated system of social laws.

Here, in the United States, what splendid work might be done if only measures of industrial and social reform could be lifted above the plane of party politics! What an object lesson America

2 A

might be to the whole commercial world if only she would refuse to subordinate questions concerning the general welfare of the public to political strife.

But no one can look into the political arena to-day without feeling that men of all political creeds are getting closer together in these big questions dealing with the industrial life of the country; and I for one believe that the United States has it in her power to remedy this social and industrial trouble. She has the key to the secret lock, let her turn it in the wards, and bring forth her magic cure for the grievances and complaints from which the social organism is so severely suffering.

2. Private Initiative.

This brings me to the second factor in social progress; namely, private initiative.

Private initiative has effected much, and is capable of effecting considerably more. It would be difficult to estimate the value of such activities as the Trades-unions, Coöperative Societies, National Temperance Leagues, National Associations for the Prevention of Consumption, Labour Unions, and other kindred organizations. Then, enumerate, if you can, all the Philanthropic and Charitable Institutions, such as Settlements,

Clubs, Homes, which are scattered throughout the old countries, notably in England.

If the rich are rich for the sake of the poor, and the poor poor for the sake of the rich, then, here in these multitudinous Settlements dotted up and down the slumdoms of our mammoth London metropolis, you will see how many of the well-to-do make use of the good things of this world by sharing them with their needy brothers and sisters.

But besides these charitable institutions to which I refer, let me point out the service being done to the toiling classes by coöperative business concerns, by coöperation in the distribution as well as in the production of economic goods. Then there is the profit-sharing business by which the employee receives a share of any profit made by the employer beyond bare interest on capital.

These profit-sharing and labour copartnership systems have on the whole worked well in England. Livesey, of Liverpool; Hartley, of Aintree; Clarke-Nicholls and Combs of London; J. T. Taylor, of Batley, not to mention other firms, and numerous British Gas Companies, give their men an interest in their businesses. Profit-sharing and copartnership introduce the much-needed *human element* into business; they bring employer and employee into closer relationship, and they make Capital and Labour interested in the financial success of the same commercial enterprise.

This method of doing business has given a setback in many districts to Socialism, and has made men take pride in their firms, and put heart into their work.

The plan of profit-sharing that is most generally adopted not only in England, but in the United States also, is the "cash bonus." "The portion of the profits to be divided," to put the case roughly, "is paid to the employees in proportion to their wages, or salaries, and the number of hours' work for the year."

There is another new departure that has been very generally taken up by firms in the United States, and promises to work wonders for a better understanding between employer and employee — I refer to what is known as "Welfare Work," which includes an ample provision of all that is needed to put human conditions into business life. It would be impossible for me to give even a partial list of business houses where really splendid opportunities of recreation and self-improvements are offered to their wage-earners. Throughout the States I have seen, to my ever growing amazement and delight, business establishment after business establishment furnished with well-set-up club-rooms, libraries, recreation centres, wash rooms, rest rooms, dining halls, and what not for the convenience, comfort, and uplifting of employees. Not satisfied with all this I have found in the States a growing wish on the part of the heads of great firms to refine and beautify their factories, and so to rob industrial life of its deadly dull monotony. How humanizing is this! My observations here have led me to the conclusion that in the United States the employer gets closer to his employee than his brother does in the old country. The human element, of which I make so much, is more in evidence in America than in England. Capital and labour are nearer to shaking hands, to chatting with each other, and to wishing each other good-luck and God-speed.

But alas! even after a social conscience of some kind has been created, after many legislative measures have been passed, and private enterprises have been launched with the object of improving the environment and of uplifting the social and industrial conditions of the wage-earning classes, we have mournfully to confess that we seem to be nearly as far off from a solution of the Industrial Problem as when we first started out with such good will a hundred years ago. During the past week I came across a case illustrating what I mean. A lad, ten years ago, was given a job out of compassion on one of the leading dailies in this great country. He started in the mail room and passed on thence to become office boy, and on again to counter clerk, and from that to subscription-solicitor, till, at the close of his tenth year of service, he has become advertising solicitor with an excellent salary. He is dissatisfied, and wants to leave and to better himself. He imagines he has not been treated fairly, that he should already be higher up the newspaper ladder, and be given a higher wage for his very ordinary services.

If we did not personally come across intances such as this one would be disposed to think they were inventions of a diseased brain. Let me cite another example, showing how utterly impossible it is to rely on environment to create content in a wrong-headed man. I was travelling on a train and got into conversation with one of the company's servants. He was getting 106 dollars a month as a brakeman. Soon he would be promoted from brakeman to the post of freight conductor with 140 dollars a month, he had no doubt but before very long after that he would find himself nominated passenger conductor of a Pullman train with 180 or 200 dollars a month. When he retired from the service he would find a pension awaiting him. Meanwhile he was treated with the greatest consideration by his employers. He worked only fifteen days in the month, and not more than 150 hours all told. He took his meals in the dining car, could order what he willed, and paid not more than a quarter. He looked the picture of health, and ought to have been thankful beyond measure for his lot in life. He was not an educated man; he was just a handy, ready, unskilled workman to whom his employers had been considerate and kind. Was my friend contented, was he grateful? No, he would quit the company's service as soon as he could, and declared there was "nothing doing" where he was.

When employers of labour find, in return for their schemes of copartnership, profit-sharing, and the rest of it, a disposition on the part of their men, with the very first opportunity, to go on strike; when Capital taking Labour by the hand promotes it steadily, surely, with one result only, that Labour, waxing strong, revolts and kicks, it is no wonder that employers should sometimes lose heart, or grow soured, feeling they are up against a proposition which not even the very best will in the world can solve and straighten out. But we must all bear up and be resolved in season and out of season, in good and in evil repute, to do our best to make what is wrong right, and to leave as little excuse as possible for any appeal for the paid agitator whose mission it would seem is to create grievances which defy redress.

What we need, again let me say it, is the wide diffusion of a social sense. We expend a considerable amount of energy on electioneering and party politics, but how many of us will lift a finger to coöperate in that social reform which should be raised far above the turmoil of party?

It is not only measures we want, but men to work them. Disinclination to take part in the work of social reform is found to characterize the majority of our people from the top rung to the bottom. The workers are the exception, and they have to contend with a mountain of apathy and indifference. The rich, with noble exceptions, are absorbed in pleasure hunting; the middle class are sunk in routine; the toilers are engaged in the grim fight for daily bread. Social responsibility fails to make itself felt. A general or local election, with its torrent of rhetorical platitudes, special pleading and windy sentiment, its scarcely concealed briberies, its gross exaggerations, and its coloured news, will for a few weeks secure the public attention. But a general election is not a time when a sound civic sense is calculated to develop. And when it is past we revert to our former ways.

Social reform is not a thing that can be put into commission with a stroke of the pen. It postulates a widespread social sense. It is a matter in which we must all be interested, and to which we must all in one way or another contribute.

3. The Action of the Church.

And now I come to that factor in social reform which is so often left out of account, and which the Socialist almost invariably ignores or depreciates; I mean the influence of Christianity.

And if I speak more particularly of the Catholic Church, let it not be thought that I undervalue the Christian social action of those who are outside its fold. I believe that Christianity exists in its fullness and integrity in the Roman Catholic Church and in it alone. But I have nothing but praise and admiration for the social action of those who, though deprived of the fulness of Christian teaching, are yet embodying Christianity, as they know it, in generous efforts for the amelioration of the people's miseries. But I must be allowed to speak of the Catholic Church, since it is her doctrine more particularly that I seek to explain in these Conferences, and it is her action in this and other lands with which I am most familiar.

Catholic writers have ever insisted on the fact that Christianity must be the basis of true social well-being. They do not mean by this that the Church alone can effect such well-being: for in the Catholic view the State has positive functions to discharge in ameliorating the condition of the people. Neither do they mean that social well-being and temporal prosperity are the ultimate ends for which the Church exists. But what they do mean is that the social question cannot be solved apart from the Church, since the Church, in Newman's phrase, supplies "the binding principle of society."

The Catholic Church protests against current Capitalism with its unmoral or immoral economies, its false boast of freedom, its undisguised utilitarianism. She protests against Socialism which, in the ultimate analysis, is equally utilitarian. To both she says: "In cutting yourselves off from me you are cutting yourselves off from what is most sound in European tradition. You are cutting yourselves off from a great spiritual force, without which society can make no real progress." Legislative machinery and economic ordinances cannot give men ideals, or permanently and effectively check their greed, or teach the dignity and duty of labour, or maintain that purity of child life and of family life upon which social well-being depends. The Church can do all these things. Hence the Church is a necessary factor in social progress.

I am speaking of modern times. I am not speaking of ancient civilizations or remote lands where Christianity has not yet secured a foothold. The people of Europe and America, like Constantine, have seen the cross in the sky, and can never be as though they had seen it not. Pre-Christian civilizations may have attained to some measure of well-being by cultivating the merely natural virtues. They groped for the truth and guided themselves by broken lights. If we, who have the fulness of light, turn away from it, our darkness will be complete. "The ' after-Christian,'" writes Devar, "cannot attain even the measure of success that lay open to the 'fore-Christian.' "

What then should be the attitude of a wise and just government to the Historic Church of Christ? What should be the attitude toward that Church of the various forms of public and private social initiative which, as I have shown, are necessary to supplement social legislation?

I do not now speak of the divine claims of the Catholic Church. I do not raise the question of the ideal relations which should subsist between the religious and the civil powers. I take lower ground, and consider what, as a mere matter of expediency, and having in view the public welfare, should be the attitude of the Civil Power to the Catholic Church. I appeal even to those who have no understanding of or sympathy with our dogmatic position.

The Catholic Church can evoke forces which the State is incapable of producing. Dealing as she does with the human conscience, she can make an intimate appeal to the heart of man which is beyond the power of any civil government. The Church which brings man into direct and supernatural relations with his Maker, can implant in him a basic principle of right living and a foundation of social service which no government can create. The Church fosters those virtues without which high civic life becomes impossible. Hence, for the State to cripple the Church, to meddle with her inward constitution, to hamper her freedom of action, is suicidal.

Nothing can take her place. To repress her action is to tamper with the delicate springs upon which the State itself rests. A secular State develops an irrational panic at the supposed menace to patriotism involved in the doctrine, say, of the Immaculate Conception, or of Papal Infallibility, or some other Catholic dogma. Catholic schools are banned or hampered, Catholic public worship rendered difficult or impossible. The social influence of the clergy is restricted, the charitable activity of the Church impeded. What is the result? We have seen it in many European countries often enough during the last half century. Public morality suffers, sanctions are removed, ideals are dimmed. The State finds that it has raised up for itself a host of evils with which it cannot cope. Again and again we have been presented with the spectacle of a bigoted government expending its energies on the suppression of dogma which it does not even understand. It neglects its proper work of promoting the people's temporal welfare in order to ruin their spiritual well-being. But the people who are thus emancipated from their reverence for God cease to retain their reverence for the state. The neglect of God's law leads to the neglect of human law. Passions are unchained and all authority is imperilled.

Governments sometimes let loose forces which they cannot control. When they turn God, the Moral Lawgiver, out of their public schools, they find revelations which astound our Juvenile Courts. They seek a remedy. They introduce "Moral Hygiene," or "Lay Morality" into the schools.

But without God at the back of a law it fails when most needed. During the year of the big famine in Ireland there was no record of a single suicide; last year in the United States there were no less than 15,000 cases of self-slaughter, and 100,000 divorces! Are we going to try and run a great Republic without God!

Again, sometimes a government becomes obsessed with the pernicious idea that State interference should be pressed to its utmost limits in education, poor relief, and so forth. Let there be no schools but government schools, no orphanages save government orphanages, no poor relief save government poor relief. What is the result? The result is much bickering and strife and no real progress in education, poor relief, or any other social function. Wise men see the danger and the folly of attempting to cripple the spiritual forces upon which national well-being depends. They deprecate religious persecution even though they do not share the religious faith which is persecuted. Let me quote the words of one of our foremost educational authorities in England, Professor Sadler : —

"The denominational schools would be the means of preserving the educational and moral tradition which has grown out of a religious way of life, and which appeals to many temperaments (though not to all) as does no other character-forming influence in education. It is in these schools too that the teaching of the organized religious bodies, in its application to the needs of young people, would find continuity and development. . . .

"For the nation to adopt the policy of privileged secularism would be to miss a great opportunity. England may, if she wishes, set an example to the world in the generosity and efficiency of her educational system. She, as can no other great nation, may unite in tolerant synthesis diverse types of school and diverse kinds of educational influence, and in this, as in other branches of public policy, preserve by a bold combination of opposites her historical continuity and her public peace." (Presidential Address to the Teachers' Guild, 1909.)

These are wise words, inspired by a true patriotism. They are the words of one who is zealous for true social well-being, irrespective of creed or country. As in education, so in poor relief, State action is called for, but such action must not be employed to stifle the initiative that springs from religious conviction. If it is, then the government which claimed to do all will find that its task has grown beyond all possibility of fulfilment. The French government turns out the nuns from the hospitals — and finds itself constrained to employ the services of convicts as nurses. The French government grasps at the thousand million of the congregations. The sum is discovered to be non-existent; but the French government finds itself charged with the care of the thousands of helpless children and sufferers who were previously given shelter and education by the Congregations. This is scarcely social progress.

Even well-intentioned Socialists in every country are apt to have the same prejudice in favour of unification, the same suspicion of private religious enterprise. Even when they accept it as inevitable for the present, they regard it as a temporary expedient, to be superseded in time by State action. Catholics regard the social function of their religion as a permanent function. A greater or less degree of State inspection and control may be necessary; but the Catholic spirit must always embody itself in educational, reformatory and charitable institutions of one kind or another. That is a permanent social need.

The Catholic spirit has so embodied itself in England and in the United States. It is making a solid and valuable contribution to the solution of the social question. I have already spoken of the numerous Catholic institutions which exist for the direct alleviation of temporal misfortunes. They embody an amount of self-sacrifice, of personal service, of wise and economical administration, of true insight into human needs which could not be supplied by an army of government officials. If we Catholics have not that proportion of lay social workers among us which might be expected, it is largely because those, who, if they belonged to other religious bodies, would become lay social workers, as a matter of fact with us become members of religious orders. Hence their work is not so much in the public eye; yet it is lifted into a higher plane and gains in those qualities which give social work its value.

But let us penetrate more deeply into the secret of the social work which the Catholic Church is carrying on in countries on both sides the

2 B

Atlantic. What is its mainspring? Is it inspired by ideals of mere temporal prosperity? or has it an intrinsic value of its own not to be found in the ideals of time?

The greatest statesmen in all ages have understood and prized the social force, the social cohesion, and the stimulus to duty which spring from the Catholic conception of life. Constantine knew it; Napoleon knew it; Washington knew it; present-day statesmen in the United States know it. It is the second-rate politician who ignores it. The Catholic Church is the stay and support of States, the abiding foundation of civic duty and social service. Belief in the Fatherhood of God creates the Brotherhood of man. Reverence for God's authority implies reverence for that authority which God has delegated to civil rulers. No purely "rational" grounds for civic obedience and social service have yet been discovered. St. Augustine long ago pointed to the beneficent influence of the Church.

"Let those who say that the doctrine of Christ is adverse to the State . . . show us an army of soldiers such as the doctrine of Christ has commanded them to be, let them show us such governors of provinces, such husbands and wives, such parents and children, such masters and servants, such kings, such judges as the Christian teaching would have them to be, nay, such contributors of all manner of taxes and such gatherers of taxes; and then let them have the face, if they can, to tell us that such teaching is injurious to the State." (Ep. 138 ad Marcellinum.)

Truth to tell, with us Catholics patriotism is something more than a sentiment, a tradition. It is a growth of our creed. It is that rare, rich bloom whose roots lie buried deep in the virgin soil of our holy religion. Hence the words so often quoted: "The better the Catholic the better the citizen." Secularists may try to snatch the flower from the stem and decorate their own philosophy with it, but the flower will wither. It needs its native soil.

The Catholic Church is doing an enormous social work in the United States and in England either directly by means of her own children, or indirectly by means of those who retain some part of her beliefs and her traditions. Such work is a great national asset; to trifle with it would be to provoke national disaster.

And if you point to Catholics who are making no contribution to social welfare — to Catholics who either give themselves up to self-indulgence and ease, or have fallen below the line of efficiency and occupy our prisons and reformatories — then I answer that these men have failed not because of their Catholicism, but in spite of it. And I would ask our critics to remember the heavy social disabilities which still press upon Catholics in so many forms in the old country. We are still to a large extent ostracized. Our children are shut out from educational advantages which are within the reach of others; our professional men still find, in too many cases, that their faith is a bar to their advancement. Moreover, the numbing effects of a far more severe persecution still remain with us. Give us a chance, give us time, give us fair play, and you will see that St. Augustine spoke truth, and that the Catholic spirit is society's best asset.

Certainly no body of men, no organization on this earth is so whole-heartedly loyal to its flag as Catholics are. In the United States, from the Hudson to the Yukon, is stretched one long line of Catholic American citizens loyal and true to the Stars and the Stripes; and from the Golden Gates in the south to the Arctic Circle in the north there is drawn up another line for defence of country, equally brave, equally strong. What a matchless force is the Old Church! Fifteen millions and more of citizens recruited into one mighty army, all inspired by the same faith, all actuated by the same motives in this land stretching from the Atlantic to the Pacific! Be sure, that if ever a last shot, which God avert, were to be fired for the Star-spangled Banner, the man to fire it would be not a Socialist, but a Catholic.

Such, then, is the Catholic solution of the social question, — the Church, the State, and Private Initiative working in harmonious concord. It would be going beyond my province to state what in detail should be the reforms undertaken by the Triple Alliance formed by the united action of Church, State, and Private Enterprise. But this much I may venture to say, that no concerted action of any kind can be effective and lasting in its results unless it becomes penetrated and permeated with the spirit of Christian justice and Christian charity. I say penetrated and permeated not merely with justice as laid down in law books, but as written on the tablets of the heart, in the Gospel of Christ, and in the spirit of His teaching. Nor is this enough without its association with the Charity of Christ, for without this interior law of charity, justice may strike too hard a bargain to satisfy human nature as actually it is constituted.

Instead, then, of going on to Socialism with all

its blindness to consequences destructive of social and industrial well-being, let us come back to Christ with His laws adjusting relations between Capital and Labour.

Christ, I say, and Christ only, can be Arbitrator in the case before us, in the conflict between Larger Dividends and Higher Wages.

If only employers and employees were to heed Christ's ruling, they would both begin to realize that there can be no permanent settlement of the industrial problem till they both alike accept His principles of justice, equity, and charity. My final word, then, to all persons interested in the social and industrial problems of the day is this:—

To employers I would say: Rally to the standard of Christ, the civilized world's Great Reformer, Inspirer, and Liberator. Exchange the rivalry between wealth and wages for a fairer division of the profits. Instead of making exorbitant profits your aim, let profit-sharing be your ambition. Come once more to realize that the Fatherhood of God means a Brotherhood inspired and actuated by a spirit of justice and charity manifesting itself in sympathy, patience, and forbearance with all men. You are only the stewards of God. One day you will have to give an account of your goods.

You will have to give an account of how you shared them with the men who helped you win them.

To wage-earners, men and women, I would say: You have a right to form unions and by means of unions to enforce your just demands for a living wage and human conditions both in your workshops and in your homes.

But there is a word of warning which you must let me add : it is a word which I utter as a friend of the workingman, as a friend who in season and out of season has lifted his voice in behalf of the toiling masses, and who during these Conferences has had nothing more at heart than to win a hearing for the toilers. That word of warning is : in your labour unions, in your disputes with your employers, nay, even in the sad necessity of a strike, never, never commit yourselves to the leadership of men who are the enemies of Christ and who, if true to their principles, must rob you of the dearest possession you have, your Christian Faith.

To all I would say, no matter what our position and work in life may be, let us make it our ambition, as it is our mission, to teach all the world that we all have a common origin and a common destiny; that the same human nature in us has the same yearnings for peace, rest, and happiness; that we all have the same Saviour, that in less than no time our present differences will vanish like a dream, and that then, if we be worthy, shadows will give place to realities, faith shall pass into vision, hope shall be more than realized, and all men will discover that the conflicts of time were meant to be victories for eternity, and the rivalry of the Brotherhood, a rivalry of service in the interests of our common Father in Heaven, whose Home and whose love shall be ours throughout the everlasting day of Eternity.

INDEX

2 c

THE following pages contain advertisements of works by Abbot Gasquet, D.D., O.S.B.